I wonder if lawnmowers can swim?

Roger Day

CHARIS BOOKS

Published in the United Kingdom by:
Charis Books, 1a Forum Buildings
Bath, Avon BA1 1UG, UK

A catalogue record for this book
is available from the British Library

Production Services by MTL: 0117 9312903

Typeset, printed and bound in the United Kingdom

I wonder if lawnmowers can swim?

Contents

Acknowledgments		7
Foreword by Steve Chalke		9
1	Taking risks	11
2	Gentle giant	20
3	Timothy David	30
4	Homeward bound	34
5	The Day of the Vow	39
6	Ups and downs of family life	44
7	Together again	58
8	A sudden stop	66
9	Diary of an 18-year-old	70
10	Help on its way	82
11	Guinness scented socks	85
12	Fearsome foursome	91
13	Smelly Egypt	97
14	Laughing landlady	102
15	Saxophone busker	109
16	Long road home	113
17	Party on!	114
18	Keeping watch	122
19	Nkosi Sikelele Afrika!	124
20	Ready to return	134
21	No fear!	139
22	Early morning shock	150
23	Who will fill these boots?	153
24	What he meant to me	159
25	Working at the bar	181
	Postscript	184

Acknowledgments

Any book is the product of more than one person. Many others have been involved in making this book possible, and I would like to acknowledge their help and encouragement.

First, thanks to all Simon's friends, acquaintances and work colleagues for their hundreds of anecdotes and funny stories. A special thanks to James Porter, who was willing to share deep secrets from his close companionship with Simon.

I would like to thank my researcher, Naomi Hill, for her careful and diligent work. Thanks also goes to David Hansford for his commitment to excellence in the design, presentation and production.

An author is only as good as his critics. I've appreciated the constructive criticisms and encouraging comments made on the manuscript by David Matthew and Erica Briedenhann. My thanks, too, to my wife Christine, who combines the role of greatest encourager and biggest critic.

Above all, I want to thank the Reynolds family—Peter, Barbie, Sarah, Dave, Daniel, Susie and Jonathan. Through their willingness to put many hours into talking about the fun times and painful memories and to share Simon's private letters and writings they have greatly enhanced this book.

Roger Day

Foreword

The story of Simon Reynolds is one of a young man who took risks for God.

Not content to sit in church and wait for people to come along, Simon went out into the streets and befriended them—tramps, buskers, young people. He gave them meals, welcomed them into his home and took them along to church meetings.

He saw many injustices in society. But instead of merely sitting back or protesting, he decided to do something about it. He spent six months visiting South African townships and squatter camps as an 18-year-old, then returned to South Africa when he was 20 to identify with South Africans of all races.

On one occasion, township youths told him he'd be burned alive if he didn't leave. 'I didn't come here to be burned,' he declared boldly. 'I came here to tell people about Jesus.'

When he saw a six-year-old Coloured boy pushing his little bike late at night, he brought him home, put him in his own bed for the night, then took him 150 km home to his mother.

Simon took risks with his life as a bouncer at a hotel bar in the Cape. In his desire to identify with people of all races he was threatened with guns and beaten by drunken gangs. His fellow bouncer said he didn't need to talk about God. 'Simon showed us how to live—and I just wanted to be like him.'

I commend this book to young and old. Read it and you will never be the same again.

Simon's crazy, wild yet godly life will challenge young people to action.

The fact that he was a difficult child and moody teenager, yet turned out to be an example to thousands of people around the world, will encourage parents who despair of their growing children.

Older people will be inspired by his story to pray for the up-and-coming generation to have an impact on the world.

'Risks must be taken,' wrote Simon, 'because one of the greatest dangers in life is to risk nothing . . . Only a person who risks all that he cannot keep, to gain what he can never lose, is truly free.'

Steve Chalke
Oasis Trust

1

Taking risks

To laugh is to risk looking a fool.
To weep is to risk appearing sentimental.
To reach out for another is to risk involvement.

To show feelings is to risk revealing your true self.
To place your ideas and dreams before a crowd is to
*   risk their loss.*

To love is to risk rejection.
To live is to risk dying.
To hope is to risk despair.
To try is to risk failure.

But risks must be taken,
Because one of the greatest dangers in life is to risk
*   nothing.*
Those who risk nothing do nothing, achieve nothing
*   and become nothing.*
They may avoid suffering and sorrow,
But they cannot learn, feel, change, grow, love or even
*   live.*
Chained by their uncertainties, they are slaves.
They have forfeited their freedom.
Only a person who risks all that he cannot keep,
To gain what he can never lose,
Is truly free.

For Simon Reynolds, taking risks was a part of
everyday life. He wrote his poem *Risk* after coming
across a short anonymous poem that inspired him. He
added things to it, reshaping it into exactly what
expressed his feelings about his forthcoming trip to South
Africa. He'd already spent six months in that country as a

teenager and had returned to Britain to prepare himself for a much longer trip—perhaps for life.

Simon was aware that, with the political turmoil in 1992, there was a serious element of risk in returning to such a volatile country. But he reckoned it was worth it.

As he guessed, things weren't easy. He wrote back home from the farm where he was staying:

The violence has definitely got worse since I was here last. Just this little town of Richmond, near Durban, has had United Nations trucks patrolling it this last week. Probably about half the white owned houses in Richmond now have high electric fences surrounding the grounds.

Despite criticism from some of his Christian friends, Simon worked in the evenings as a bouncer at a hotel bar in Somerset West. At the bar there were fights most nights. Simon saw his job there as much more than a chance to earn some money. For him, working at a bar that drew young people from across the races was a part of the risk he took to bring justice to what he saw as still an unjust society. He wrote:

Actively standing for justice is not merely a right we have. For us as Christians it's an obligation. I'm proud to be in a position where I can bring justice to injustice in my job at the bar.

I watch the thugs get drunk, then throw their physical and verbal weight around, intimidating all who listen. I watch the big guy beat the small guy to impress the now terrified small guy's girl. I thank God for my large size. To the big guy I'm the big guy.

Deep in my heart I have no moral problem working there. Some people in the church think I'm wrong because it's wrong to fight. When I fight I'm fighting for someone who can't fight for himself. People have apparently been killed in that bar. I know the barman was shot dead six months ago.

Something about a black (African) man in this culture is that when he sets his mind to kill, he won't stop till he does. So you then get some drunk, loud-mouthed white or Coloured (Brown) man who insults or threatens the black guy and there's a fight. The white or Coloured guy sobers up fast and he knows this black guy is going to kill him. So he fights with all he's got to save his own neck. When no one breaks up the fight, nine times out of ten someone dies.

This last Saturday has made me think a little harder. There was a huge white guy about 6'3" with a big build. He had long, shaggy blond hair and arms thick like legs. He came to the bar alone and was being a general pain to a group of Coloured people who were all visibly afraid. He was drunk or getting there. He kept asking me for a fight, which made me nervous because he was such a big guy.

Eventually the two of us had had enough. I said to the barman in front of the guy, 'No more drink for him.'

Enraged, the guy turned and punched the nearest guy he could see, who happened to be a Coloured guy we know. He was about 40, sober, sitting on a stool talking to his wife. He fell off the stool and the big guy jumped on him. We grabbed him and shocked him with the stun gun (6000 volts). He didn't even fall over! He just shouted and ran at us both. We punched him in the face, three or four times each until he fell. It was like he wasn't human. If you hit them right, most people go down after one punch—two or three at the most.

On the floor he tried to grab us. We shocked him some more, but it was no good. So we punched him until he was unconscious. I've seen people freak out in there, but this guy just seemed to want to kill anything. We couldn't hold him down or still. He was too strong. We threw a bucket of water over him.

This went on for over half an hour. We'd drag him outside, then he'd find strength from somewhere and jump up and lash out. It took three of us—me, Alastair and the owner—to keep him under control. We just punched him until he fell, every time he went for us.

After three-quarters of an hour the police and an ambulance came. I took Alastair to hospital because he'd broken his hand. I bruised my hand and got a cut on my eye. I visited the big guy in hospital after church but they said he'd run away, probably for fear of the police.

I'm haunted with questions like, 'Will he live?' 'Will he be brain damaged?' 'Will he come back for revenge?' He'll certainly never look the same.

The positive side of working there is the people I meet. There have been so many people I've been able to tell about Jesus Christ and what he does for me.

I asked God for a job and this is what he gave me. Am I wrong? I'm living in a violent time, working in a violent bar in a violent country. I don't plan to quit just because it's rough or scary. I'll quit if I see it's not the place where God wants me to be.

Things didn't improve at the bar. In a later letter to his parents he wrote:

I've lost count of the number of knives pulled on me over the past eight months. I carry a dagger with a six-inch blade when working, but I've only once ever pulled it out and fortunately didn't have to use it. I've had people come at me with truncheons, twice a chain and once a panga (like a samurai sword). Every now and again people smash bottles and use the broken ends as weapons.

About six week ago a guy chased me with an AK47 rifle machine gun. Last Tuesday night at about 1.00 am I went out to the car park just to check it and found a drunk guy fumbling in his bag. I asked if I could help him and he pulled out a pistol and held it to my head. He told me to 'f . . . off' and then walked away. It gave my heart-beat a good bit of exercise!

Late in November 1993 he stopped working at the hotel bar. He felt relieved that it was over. Looking back, he strongly believed that God had used that job to expose him to an aspect of the world he'd never have experienced otherwise.

One Sunday night there had been a shooting at the Anglican church in Cape Town. It was a tragedy to those involved, a terrifying enigma to those who viewed the aftermath. Up until then he hadn't really feared for his safety in terms of racial violence. But several times recently he'd woken at night scared, just thinking about how the brutal, senseless violence was increasing in South Africa.

His work in the townships continued. For a time he was working with two black guys from Khayalitsha township near Cape Town. He was standing in for another guy who was ill. This man, together with three labourers, had recently been held up at gunpoint there.

A stretch of the N2 motorway from Somerset West to Cape Town had a five-kilometre section on it that had become known as the Hell Run. It went right alongside Khayalitsha township. Extremist black young people would throw bricks at cars from the side of the road. They concentrated on white people. Many travellers had been killed or injured over the past few months. The extremists also shot at cars and even at planes landing at the airport runway, which was literally across the road from the township.

Simon had to drive down the Hell Run three or four times a day. The scariest thing for him was that the extremists would tie a long rope to a rock and, as a car was driven at up to 120 km (70 mph) under the bridge, they would swing the rock down through the car windscreen. Every time Simon saw someone standing on a bridge over the highway he was driving on he would spontaneously start praying.

Soldiers now lined the Hell Run 24 hours a day, with foot patrols on every bridge and up and down both sides of the road. But the extremists even shot at the soldiers. Teams of soldiers consisting of 10 to 15 men would ride on scrambler bikes around the area, all in single file. Simon wrote:

> When you see that kind of thing you just have to stop and wonder what's going on here. We've really screwed up this world.

Simon was driving to a job one Thursday on a long, straight country road. As he came through a small settlement he went past a group of young black guys on the side of the road. One of them picked up a small rock and threw it at the *bakkie* (pick-up truck). Fortunately ('Or was it God?' Simon asked later) it came at such an angle that the force wasn't enough to break the windscreen, but bounced across the screen and fell off. It gave him a fright, though, and his right foot seemed to increase in weight against the accelerator.

Another time a 22-year-old guy from the bar was looking after a house for friends. He came home to find some black men robbing the house. Police said he was tortured for about half an hour before being stabbed to death through the heart by a two-foot long *panga*.

Another pointless death, soon to become just another statistic of a forgotten life buried under the blood of a revolution that the majority of the people don't want. What a mess!

Simon, together with his friends Deon Briedenhann and Daniel van Eeden, were eating supper at about 7 pm one night when the phone rang. Deon answered to a lady in hysterics. All she could say was, 'He's trying to get in! He's trying to get in!'

Deon calmly asked her where she was and got her address. Then he asked, 'Why are you ringing me?'

It turned out that she thought she'd rung the police but in her panic had dialled the wrong number. Deon told her to put the phone down and call the police and that he and his friends were on their way.

The three of them were there within three and a half minutes, speeding through town and jumping every red light. With one gun between them they checked every room of the old farmhouse where the lady lived. Hearts pounding, they searched the grounds, but could find nothing. They could only assume they'd scared the man off. The lady showed them the bedroom window he'd smashed and said she'd watched him trying to get in. The shocking thing was, it took the police half an hour to arrive.

Simon believed there was another frightening truth about this incident. The police weren't being slow or lazy; they were busy risking their lives somewhere else. Police died like flies in South Africa so few people now wanted to be a policeman. The result was that there weren't enough of them to keep the peace.

Simon wrote to his parents:

There is without doubt a need for good policemen in South Africa, people who will stand and implement justice, regardless of the personal cost. Please don't spread this too widely, but I briefly considered training

as a police officer here. This place is full of injustice,
bullying, terrorising, the rich capitalising on the fear of
the poor. The countless incidents we come up against
are all reflections of the country as a whole.

Simon was told firmly by local Christian leaders not to
go into Lwandle or Khayalitsha townships alone. But he
often forgot his own safety in his desire to identify with
township people.

I'm scared of a lot of things in life—vicious dogs,
horses, sharks, etc—but God seems to have barred all
fear of township violence from me. The reason is
obvious to me. He wants me in the townships. I know
he's not sending me there to die. Anyway, I love being
with those guys. They make me laugh so much.
I'd be lying to tell you I don't have freaky moments.
But I always know deep down that God's with me. It's
vitally important not to respond to fear. We must learn
to obey instinctively in a panic situation.

Just three weeks before he arrived to work at Lwandle
squatter camp, four young white men had gone into a
store in the camp to buy liquor. Two were burned alive
with bicycle tyres filled with petrol wrapped around their
necks. One had his tongue cut out and was left to bleed
to death. The fourth escaped to tell the grisly tale.

A while later Simon visited a nearby squatter camp,
Sun City. He went alone because he couldn't find anyone
to go with him. After he wandered around for an hour,
two young blacks came up to him.

'You must leave here, man,' one of them said.

'Why?'

'There are people from Lwandle here today and they'll
burn you alive if they see you.'

'I didn't come here to be burned,' Simon replied
instinctively. 'I came here to tell people about Jesus.'

The two guys shook their heads and walked off.

I told God, 'If you brought me here to tell people about
you, who should I tell?' Just then I walked past a
shabeen *(a bar) made of corrugated iron and*
cardboard. I walked in and met the owner, who spoke

quite good English. It turned out he's the African
National Congress (ANC) chairman for Sun City.

Anyway, the long and short of it is, I got him to
translate while I told three men there about Jesus, two
of whom gave their lives to Christ. The owner, Eugene,
thinks he's already a Christian. I think not, but we'll let
him be for a while. He was so excited when I prayed
for these two men.

Afterwards he said he would fill the shabeen *with*
people if I'd come back and tell them about Jesus.
We've arranged it for 7 pm tonight. Now, what if I'd
listened to my fear when those two guys told me to
leave?

I went back again today to remind Eugene but he
wasn't there. I was greeted by people around the
township who were saying, 'Tonight at the shabeen*!'*
I'm quite excited but very nervous.

After the meeting at the *shabeen* Simon wrote:

Twenty-seven people came. I'm picking some of them
up for church on Sunday. And they want another
meeting next week. Party on!

During his regular visits to Sun City, Simon made a lot
of friends and some enemies. He often went there alone
as he felt he was less of a threat that way.

So far eight people have been converted to Jesus
Christ, including the ANC chairman and his mother and
sister. However, I've now run into problems with his
father, who has just returned home from a trip. He
doesn't want me in there and he won't let any of those
eight new Christians come to church. So now I'm trying
to organise a weekly Bible study meeting in a
neighbouring township. I've found a hut big enough to
meet in and a lady who lives there has agreed to let us
use it. We can only have the meetings at night because
the people work in the day.

It'll be risky but worth it. It seems that anything
really worth having you have to risk something to
obtain.

As a 21-year-old in South Africa, Simon was without a doubt a young man who took risks for God. But as a child he was no angel.

2

Gentle giant

Simon Nathan Reynolds was born on 19 August 1972. He and his family lived on a housing estate in a tiny two-bedroom council house in Bath. Although at 8lb 2oz (3686 gm) he weighed only slightly more than average, he had enormous hands and feet.

According to his parents, he was generally a happy, contented baby. His sister, Sarah, was only 16 months older than him. From birth, she adored him and would coo over him and play with him whenever she could.

As he grew, he always seemed to be one step ahead of other babies in his physical development. Within a few weeks he'd lost that tiny baby look. He surprised his parents by crawling off a double bed at 4½ months.

Soon he was crawling around the house, bumping and crashing into furniture. It didn't seem to bother him in the slightest. By five months he could crawl out of his carrycot, roaring with laughter as he saw it all as a huge joke. It wasn't long before he could get out of a cot or anything else he was put into.

Within the next couple of months he'd developed a huge appetite, a short memory concerning the word 'no' and the ability to climb all the way upstairs without help. By nine months Simon would clap his hands when he started to sing. When he went on holiday he seemed to enjoy eating handfuls of ice cream and sand mixed.

He was adventurous, always exploring new things. He had a passion for cars and tractors. When most babies and toddlers took a cuddly toy to bed, Simon wouldn't settle down until he had a Matchbox car in his fist. He'd even ask for his car in his sleep!

At 18 months he copied whole sentences of his big sister, Sarah. The intonation was perfect but the words were totally meaningless.

One picture of him at 19 months showed him, hands in pockets, strolling around as if he owned the world. His grandad on his mum's side, Alan Norrish, who was one of the founders of Bible & Medical Missionary Fellowship (now Interserve), described him at that age as, 'The boy with the million dollar feeling.'

A few months later, though, an incident happened that affected his confidence throughout his childhood and right into his adult life. He was at the top of a slide at the back of his house when a large dog ran up the steps behind him, shot through his legs and slid down in front of him. He was terrified and ever after that was frightened of dogs. Fortunately, it didn't put him off going down slides!

When he was 19 months old his baby brother Daniel was born. Simon loved his new little brother. 'I want baby,' was his constant plea to hold him. But he soon found he was crowded between big sister and little brother. He felt he needed to make his mark. He was strong willed and would often be quite disruptive. He needed to do things in his particular way, which even as a nearly two-year-old was usually unconventional.

Peter and Barbie discovered that much of the conventional guidance on disciplining a child had to go out of the window when it came to Simon. What worked for Sarah didn't work for Simon. They came to realise that each child is an individual who needs to be disciplined accordingly.

Simon was never boring. Right through his childhood, when he was cross he breathed heavily and screwed up his nose, something that seemed to amuse the rest of the family. He was always a big boy for his age and was expected to be better behaved because people thought he was so much older than he actually was.

When Simon was 2½, Frances Neale (known as Fra to the kids), came on the scene. She was a kind of auntie to the Reynolds family. An occupational therapy technician originally from the Salvation Army, she met Simon's mum Barbie and the three children at a friend's house. Soon she'd volunteered to do babysitting for the Reynolds whenever they needed help. Sometimes she'd be there four or five times a week.

Simon and Sarah had bunk beds and there was a little narrow window at the top of the wall. By standing on

Sarah's top bunk they could both manage to see the soccer grounds from the window. Often at night when Simon couldn't sleep he'd climb up on to the top bunk and they'd watch the soccer matches together.

Soon after starting babysitting, Fra caught them on the top bunk when they should have been asleep.

'Are you allowed to do this?' she demanded.

'Oh, yes, of course,' Sarah replied.

'Yes, Mummy and Daddy say we're allowed,' said little Simon.

They got away with it—but only once.

Fra was the first one the children wanted when a babysitter was needed. She'd take them to the zoo or on picnics. She'd organise bonfires and sausage sizzles. She'd tell them bedtime stories, acting out the story and getting them to follow her around the room, through imaginary jungles and along rivers.

If Mum and Dad had to be away, Fra would look after the children for a weekend or for a few days. She was part of the furniture, spent Christmases with them and lived with the family for a period of time. She described Simon as 'a bit of a gentle giant—big and tough, yet soft as two pins when he wants to be. He finds it difficult to say sorry but once you get through to that point he's soft'.

One time Simon dressed up Fra's dog, Charlie, with a blue dressing-gown and got her to walk around on her hind legs.

Simon could come up with lots of excuses why he couldn't go to bed. Fra had to be quite strict with him. He also played tricks on Fra. At bedtime he and the others would hide in cupboards, the attic or anywhere else where they could find a place to squeeze into. The trouble was, Simon found it difficult to keep quiet for very long.

From as young as he could remember, Simon preferred the floor to sleeping in a bed. 'What's wrong with sleeping on the floor?' he'd argue with his parents. He'd then make his bed on the landing.

His parents said, 'No, you can't sleep on the floor. You must sleep in your bed because it's draughty on the floor.'

So he'd retort, 'If I wrap myself up, I won't be draughty.'

They'd say, 'You'd be in the way if you slept on the landing.'

'If I sleep against the radiator I won't be in the way.'

'Well, you're going to get disturbed because people go to and fro on the landing.'

'But I don't get disturbed. I sleep deeply and nothing wakes me.' That was absolutely true.

In the end his parents conceded. Who said people had to sleep in beds? They acknowledged that sleeping in a bed was a cultural issue. Through his teens he became too big for the average bed. He was very comfortable sleeping on the floor. When he slept in other people's homes he chose to sleep on the floor, often to his hostess's concern. Even at 21, it was rare for Simon to sleep in a bed.

As a small child he also loved sleeping on the half-landing of the stairs. It was sometimes difficult to get him to go back to his room once he was stretched out there.

A strict family came to look after the children while Peter and Barbie were away. The man came upstairs and saw Simon sleeping on the half-landing.

'What are you doing there?' he demanded. 'What do you think your parents would do if they knew?'

'They'd smack me.'

'That's what I thought. Get up to your bed.'

It wasn't true, but he didn't want to fall out of favour with yet another babysitter because of his strange behaviour.

He enjoyed playschool and thrived on the cars and tractors there. Then, a month before he was four, the family moved house. Baby sister Susie was born five days after the move. Simon's strong point wasn't patience but even when Susie screamed for a feed, he showed unusual patience and care.

For his fourth birthday Simon had a red go-kart which he rode like a Formula One racing driver. He controlled it with one hand on the steering wheel and the other on the brake as he hurtled wildly down the drive doing handbrake turns around the bend into their garden.

That summer was one of upheaval and change for Simon. He found it difficult to adjust to their new home, preferring the security of the old house. He also missed having innumerable friends outside the door any time of the day.

Even at a young age, Simon had a sense of destiny that his parents actively encouraged. He'd often talk about travelling to other countries. He'd also pray for children in Africa and elsewhere.

When he was six, he and his family got up very early to go on holiday to Cornwall. Having heard about New Zealand being 12 hours ahead of Britain, Simon asked about his grandparents living in New Zealand, 'Mummy if we get up very, very, very early, will we see the people from New Zealand walking around on our streets?' He'd assumed that because they had their night-time when British people had their daytime, it must be their turn to use the streets.

During his first couple of years at school, Simon and his big sister Sarah were very close. They played together and even ate lunch side by side. They'd suddenly pop their empty crisp packets and make the whole dining hall go silent. When Simon had crackers for lunch he'd squeeze them until the margarine came through the little holes, then go round telling everyone he was having worms in his sandwiches for lunch. Later in Africa, worms really were on the menu.

One time when they were in primary school he and his best friend David Appel got in trouble for talking in class and were sent to the headteacher's office. While they waited to be seen by her they spat on the wall and had a race to see whose spit went down the wall the fastest.

Simon could burp on demand. In primary school he once had to write out dozens of times: '*I must learn to control my bodily functions.*' He thought it was hilarious.

When Sarah had to write out lines, Simon would help her to do them in the quickest way possible, one word at a time down the page!

There was a sweetie box in their kitchen and they were allowed two sweets from it when they got home from school each day.

One evening Simon said to Daniel, 'You know the sweetie box, Daniel?'

'Yes.'

'Well, I was thinking. It wouldn't be stealing if we took some sweets 'cos they're ours anyway.'

It was typical Simon logic and it resulted in their climbing up and pigging themselves out on sweets.

At a Bible Week one year he and David Appel went to the shop, took a load of sweets, ate them all and said sorry to God.

'It's all right. We can always ask Jesus to forgive us,' reasoned David.

They later confessed to their parents and were taken back to the shop to make amends.

Once, after Daniel's birthday, Simon stole some chocolates in the shape of little ducks from Daniel's room. He denied it but eventually the truth came out and he ended up being disciplined.

As a small boy he got frustrated if he couldn't have undivided attention. Growing up in a large family meant he had to share his parents' attention with four others, now that young Jonathan (Joff) had come along. Simon was introverted as a child, but when he was on his own he came to life. He later became extrovert, possibly to compensate.

Taking this into account, his parents decided to give Simon and his brothers and sisters individual attention on a regular basis. When it was Simon's turn he could choose what he wanted to do. He loved those times, choosing anything from going rowing with his dad to having a milkshake at McDonalds. Sometimes his ideas were a bit wild, such as wanting to go to New Zealand by Concorde, but generally his parents were able to steer him gently towards less ambitious adventures.

At the age of six Simon made a decision to receive Jesus Christ as Saviour and boss of his life. It wasn't a massive, dramatic decision. It was just one thing that happened to him that day, but it was the start of something new. He knew God was going to help him run his life down a new and better track. He found God as a friend, someone who was really there. He could talk to God about anything troubling him, even personal matters.

Shoba Holly came to live with the Reynolds family when Simon was about nine. She and Simon got on well. She taught him to play badminton. When he was much older, Simon and Shoba would spend a lot of time talking. One time they went to Pizza Hut. People were staring at this odd couple—the very tall young man and the much shorter older Asian woman.

Once the family went to a conference in Clevedon. The place had a swimming pool and Daniel, his younger brother, was jumping off the highest diving boards, backwards and forwards, head first, feet first. Nine-year-old Simon had the greatest difficulty jumping off the lowest board, even feet first.

His grandad watched that occasion very intently and empathised with him. He later wrote: 'When I saw you at Clevedon I said to myself, "What a sensible and sensitive young man you are! You look before you leap. You'll make a good driver one day, always using your mirror and taking good care of other road users." Start practising all the road rules on your cycle.

'Some people jump in without forethought about the consequences. Think first and then act. But of course you have to learn to jump, too. Never easy. And those who see the possible difficulties don't jump at all. You'll learn to jump just as you learned to weigh up the consequences. Practice both. Always start with easy ones and work up gradually. Later in life you'll be able to teach others to go step by step like that.'

From when he was very young, Simon took an interest in people from other countries. His family often had people from overseas and others staying with them. He was especially concerned about suffering children.

His parents wrote of him: 'Before Simon was born we had a prophecy that he would learn in his developing years and then grow into a man who would stand up for the weak and the downtrodden, those who were being wronged by others. He'd stand up for them and would do so at his own expense.'

With this in mind Simon was constantly asking and praying about going abroad. He'd say to his parents: 'Do you think I'll ever fly in a plane?'

For Simon's 10th birthday Peter took him on a short plane trip. It was a single-engined Cessna and they flew for 20 minutes over Bristol, Portishead and the Bristol Channel. Simon sat in the copilot's seat and Peter in a little seat at the back. The pilot explained to Simon all about the instruments. He also took them through a steep turn so that Simon could feel what G-force was like.

A year or so later Simon went abroad for the first time in his life. The Reynolds had a family holiday in Majorca. At long last, a lifetime dream was starting to be realised, even if it was only a holiday.

Simon spent a lot of the time pushing three-year-old Joff around in a little inflatable boat. Eventually the boat burst and Jonathan ended up in bed with severe sunstroke.

Later that day Simon was swimming and Mum called him in for a meal. Simon came tearing into shore, terror gripping him. 'What's wrong, Mum? Joff hasn't died has he?' How he loved his little brother!

Another time Simon and Susie were walking along the beach. Simon put his arm around his little sister and said, 'I'm sorry for all the horrible things I've said to you. I'm glad you're my sister.'

Throughout the holiday the children wore suntan cream each day. On the last day they pleaded with Mum that they didn't need suntan cream and they didn't mind getting burnt. She conceded but within a day both Simon and Daniel were covered in huge blisters up to six inches across.

Simon wrote after the holiday:

I enjoyed the plane ride to Majorca very much because the service was good. For instance, I could just say to one of the stewardesses, 'Please could I have some Coke?' and I could say that about five times and each time they would say, 'Certainly,' or, 'Yes, of course.' But on the way back they wouldn't offer us a drink at all. If we wanted a drink we would have to go and ask for one and after the first one if we were still thirsty and we asked for another one they would just say, 'What now?' and things like that. So I personally thought that Iberia, the first plane, was the best one.

It was very difficult to decide what I liked best in Majorca, but when I really think about it I liked swimming in the sea and the pool, going on my Lilo, watching bullfights on TV and going on the paddle boats.

Later that same year, Simon and his family went abroad again, this time to India for a month. They met up with Simon's grandparents, who were working there. They visited the home where his mum had lived throughout her childhood. They also visited Pakistan. This trip confirmed Simon's love of other countries and people of different cultures.

When Simon was 11 he and his little brother Daniel went on a camping trip. They loaded up with a tent and lots of equipment on their backs and set off from their home in Bath. They walked for miles and miles, then as it was getting dark they set up their tent in a friend's field. They got everything ready and then climbed into their sleeping bags.

As nine-year-old Daniel was settling down for the night, big brave brother Simon suddenly announced, 'I'm scared, Daniel. There's no way I can sleep here. I'm going home.'

They got out and legged it to their friend's farmhouse.

Daniel kept saying, 'It'll be all right.'

'No, it won't,' Simon replied.

The friend drove them home and they came to collect the tent the next day. Simon, the young man who could face threats from guns as an adult, was scared stiff as a child of spending a night camping.

Another time Simon and Daniel got hold of some sheets of corrugated iron and rested them against a fence. Then, while it was raining, they covered the sheets in piles and piles of mud to make the structure look like an air-raid shelter. There was mud everywhere. Then Dad came along.

'What have you done to the fence?' he demanded. 'Take it all down—now.'

They were both gutted at the fact that their carefully constructed shelter had to be destroyed. After that, they learned to ask before trying to landscape the garden!

The two boys would go off swimming, into town or shooting with Daniel's air rifle. Sometimes they'd go rowing in a boat or paddling in a canoe on the river for the day.

Susie, Daniel and Simon used to be in the same junior school. Susie wanted the day off school and asked Simon's advice to convince their parents she was ill.

'Why don't you do what I always do?'

'What's that?'

'Go up to Mum's room, get some talcum powder off her table and plaster it on your face. You have to rub it in really well. Then go and tell Mum you're ill.'

Susie went home and tried it out and it actually worked!

They had a particularly high curb outside their house. One day they were riding their bikes to school and went over the curb. Susie went over the handlebars and landed in the gutter.

Simon said, 'The only time that sort of thing happens is when God's punishing you for being naughty, so you must have done something naughty to fall off your bike.'

Ever after that, whenever anything bad happened, young Susie thought she must have done something very wrong to get punished in that way.

Years later in South Africa, Simon himself learned that God wasn't like that, even when one piece of tragic news came after another.

3

Timothy David

'Hey, Simon, phone for you.' The landlord of the hotel in remote Bophuthatswana, a self-governing state just south of Botswana, pointed to a spare handset near the reception desk.

'Y'mean me?'

'Yeah, you, Simon. Hurry up. It's all the way from England.'

'Right. I'm coming.'

Simon Reynolds pushed back his tangled mass of orange curls and stood to his full height of around 6ft 7in. No one, least of all him, knew for certain how big he was. He'd grown so tall during his teen years that he'd decided to stop measuring himself. It definitely had its advantages being so tall, especially in some of the hotspots of South Africa. At 21 but looking more like 30, Simon had a big build and a towering frame. Few people dared argue with him.

'Hello? Hello? Mum? Dad?'

'Simon!'

'Hey, Mum, it *is* you.'

'Yes, it's me, and Dad's on the other extension.'

'Cool. How'd you find me out here in the back of beyond?'

'Well, son, your boss, Deon, gave us your number. But he warned us it'd be highly unlikely we'd get you on the phone.'

'Yeah, he's right there. I wouldn't have been here if there hadn't been a hold-up in getting the paint for doing those big aerials today.'

'Really?'

'Me, Vally and the other workers are just sitting around kicking our heels until the paint's ready. And I just happened to be in reception when the call came through.

If I'd been in my room they probably wouldn't have bothered calling me to the phone.'

'Er—how are you?'

'Yeah, OK. Keeping out of mischief. Enjoying living in South Africa. You know.'

'Well, we've got some very, very sad news and we wanted to tell you before anyone else did.'

'Oh.' Simon's heart sank into his size 13 desert boots. His mind was working overtime. His grandad had died, or maybe it was one of his sisters, Sarah or Susie. Or could it be Daniel or his kid brother, Joff? Joff's real name was Jonathan, but everyone called him Joff. He smiled as he remembered just a few months ago picking up 13-year-old Joff by one hand and posing for a photo at Heathrow Airport before he left for South Africa.

'What's happened, Mum?' Simon asked at last, keeping his voice as calm as he could, despite the adrenaline pumping through his whole system.

'You know Sarah and Dave were expecting a baby?'

'Sure.' He'd always been close to his big sister Sarah and he got on well with her husband, Dave, too. Simon knew all about the baby and was really looking forward to being an uncle for the first time.

'Well, the hospital induced labour in the early hours of Thursday morning. But, sadly, the baby had already died in Sarah's womb.'

'Oh, *no!* Er—When was the baby due?'

'Any time from now on.'

'No way! I thought it was ages yet.'

'It was all going OK until three days before his birth. Sarah couldn't feel the baby moving and went to the hospital to have it checked. That's when they told her the baby's heart had stopped beating.'

'What did they do then?'

'They couldn't do a lot. They told her she'd have to go through with a normal childbirth. The only trouble was there wouldn't be a baby at the end of it. Only a body. Dave was with Sarah right through labour. It lasted 12 hours.'

'Really?'

'Dad was there during the first part of the labour, and Dave called him again as soon as the baby was born. Then Dad came to collect me from the airport. I was in the States with Susie speaking at several meetings there.'

'Yeah, I remember you telling me about that.'

'Dad took us straight to see Dave and Sarah and then we went to look at the baby in the chapel of rest.'

'Oh.'

'He was beautiful, Simon. He only weighed 5lb 9oz but he had huge hands and feet just like you when you were born. And really long legs. I'm sure he'd have ended up being another giant like you!'

Simon chuckled despite the way he felt inside.

'How are Dave and Sarah?' he asked.

'They're upset, of course, but they're OK. They've called the baby "Timothy David Entwistle". Timothy means "Honour to God" and David means "God's loved one".'

'Do they know why he died?'

'Not really. Only that his heart suddenly stopped beating.'

'Oh, I see.'

'Simon, I've got to go now. Dad and I are leading a communication workshop today. I'm sorry to have to break such sad news to you. It must be tough for you to cope with these sorts of tragedies from such a long way away. Dave and Sarah really want to talk to you, so as soon as I put the phone down I'll give them your number and they'll ring you straight back.'

'OK, I'll go up to my room and speak to them from there. It's a bit more private than here at the reception desk.'

A few minutes later, Dave and Sarah rang, still in a state of shock from their tragic bereavement.

'I'm sorry to hear about the baby, Sarah,' Simon said with feeling.

'Yeah, it's so difficult,' Sarah replied.

'Hey, Sarah,' Simon said, brightening and changing the subject, as he often did. 'I'm really having a cool time here.'

'Good.'

'I love this place, I love these people and I've decided to make South Africa my home.'

'You what? Are you sure, Simon?'

'Of course. Why? What's the problem?'

'Oh, I don't know.'

'Well, I've decided. I'll come back to England for visits, of course. But this is where I belong now. The township people especially are great. I know I'm in the right place.'

'So, tell us all your news.'

Simon continued telling Sarah about his hopes and his plans. He talked and talked, hardly letting her get a word in edgeways. Sarah was relieved that Simon changed the subject. It was as if Simon hadn't really taken in that their baby had died.

Her husband Dave took the phone from her.

'We'd better go now, Simon. We'll be in touch as soon as we can.'

'Yeah, take care of yourselves. It must be really tough for you both.'

'Thanks. Bye.'

As soon as he'd put the phone down, Simon flopped on to the bed, his legs sticking way out over the end. He sighed deeply. Sometimes he found it so difficult to show people how he felt deep inside. He'd talked and talked to Sarah as if nothing had happened, yet deep down he was hurting badly.

He knew now that tragedy was just part of life and not a judgment from God. But how could he concentrate on work when so many tragedies seemed to be happening?

4

Homeward bound

'Hey, Simon. How are you?'

'I'm OK, I suppose, Deon,' Simon replied, sprawled out on his hotel bed clutching the phone to his ear.

'Doesn't sound like it to me.'

'Well, it's just that I've recently heard some awful news.'

'What's that?'

'My nephew's been stillborn. I just can't understand why.'

'Oh, I'm sorry to hear that, Simon. What happened?'

'Dunno, really. His heart just sort of stopped before he was born.'

'That's tragic. Look, I think you need to take care of yourself.'

'What d'ya mean?'

'I think you and Vally should finish with the aerials early, cut loose and come back to the Cape straight away. We can chat things through. It seems you're under a lot of strain in such a lonely place.'

'That's right!'

'Besides, it's nearly Christmas.'

'OK, I'll come.'

Death was a subject that had come up again and again for Simon. In the nine months since he'd left England for South Africa, Simon had looked down the barrel of more than one gun. He'd been threatened in the townships, beaten almost unconscious and faced alcohol-crazed young people. Last summer, he'd written a letter to Sarah expressing his views on the subject:

I can honestly say that I'm not afraid to die. It's never tragic to die doing what you love the most. I love

*serving God and knowing I'm in South Africa where he
wants me to be and doing what he wants me to do.*

Sitting alone in his bedroom, Simon let his mind drift
back over the tragic news he'd heard that year. It was on
21 July that his grandmother had died in hospital. She'd
been frail and old. The hospital had decided to keep her
on painkillers but there was nothing more they could do
for her. Her life was waning fast and there was little point
in prolonging the agony.

But despite her massive stroke, she clung to life as if
she had some sort of unfinished business. The hospital
asked if there were any relatives who hadn't spoken with
her. Then someone thought of Simon in South Africa.
When Simon heard the news he tried ringing her, but it
was too late. She'd died two hours previously.

A month or so later he'd heard the shocking news that
his cousin Alistair, just seven weeks his junior, had died in
a microlight accident in Hungary.

Simon and Alistair had been quite close as small boys.
One time, Simon, Alistair and the other boys in the two
families had a stone throwing fight while on holiday
together in the Lake District. One stone hit Alistair on the
head and blood was gushing everywhere. They were all
worried. Simon, who was about nine, arranged with
Alistair to say that a stone had just 'ended up on his
head'! No one had actually thrown anything at him.
Alistair had to have a stitch but no one dared grass on
Simon.

Simon and Alistair became really special friends when
they were 16. Simon, his brother Daniel and sister Sarah,
along with Dave, had spent a wonderful holiday in
Greece with Alistair's family, who lived there at the time.
Throughout the holiday they'd slept on the beach in the
open air with the waves lapping almost to where they
lay.

It had been the first time the Reynolds kids had been
on holiday together without their parents. Simon smiled
as he remembered Mum's 20 or more warnings to use
suntan cream on his light, sensitive skin. Like a fool he
hadn't taken much notice. He'd sunbathed on a Lilo out at
sea and ended up with third-degree burns on the upper
part of his feet. He'd spent several days hiding from the
sun.

The thing was, he'd wanted to get brown, but he also wanted to get rid of his psoriasis. Psoriasis, a skin condition that caused flaky red patches, had dogged him throughout his childhood and into adulthood. When he was only seven while camping at a Bible Week he remembered his psoriasis flaring up. The camp doctor told him, 'This is psoriasis, all right. But you haven't got it bad, mate. And you're going to be better, you're going to be well.'

Despite that doctor's encouragement, his skin never did clear up. He remembered the embarrassment of a teacher making fun of him and kids commenting on the red patches.

He was a good swimmer but from his early teens he didn't tend to go into the water because he was so aware of the scaly patches on his body. During his first stint in South Africa he went swimming a few times, but it was still embarrassing.

He tried every form of treatment—coal tar, Alphosyl shampoo. He was interested in the fact that sunshine seemed to promote healing. He was especially aware of this when he'd been in South Africa.

Baldness ran in his family, and sometimes he wondered if he might end up with bald patches on his head clearly showing up his psoriasis. He'd grow his hair quite long to cover it up.

When it was better, he had his hair cut short. But then he was the focus of suspicion in some of the squatter camps. Because he was very white with short cropped hair, some people thought he was from the secret police. As a result, he started growing his hair long again to counter that suspicion.

The time with Alistair in Greece more than made up for the discomfort from sunburn he suffered.

Alistair Arpad Angyal had been the oldest of four children. Alistair, together with his younger brother, Joel, and their Hungarian dad, Ocsi, all had pilots' licences to fly a microlight they owned in Hungary. For Ocsi, returning to Hungary had been a dream come true. He and his brother had fled with their grandmother from the communist clampdown in 1953, crossing the border by the skin of their teeth.

Early that bright, sunny morning Alistair and his dad had gone to the airfield ready to take it in turns flying the microlight. Ocsi had been first up. Then Alistair, soaring up into the blue sky, had leaned over from the cockpit and shouted to those on the ground: 'This is *wonderful!*'

Full of confidence, Alistair tried a particularly tricky manoeuvre. Immediately, a strut on the wing snapped. The microlight nosedived, hitting the ground with a sickening thud. The two-stroke engine fell silent as the craft crumpled before their eyes. Ocsi rushed over to help him but it was too late. Alistair had been killed instantly.

Alistair died on Simon's 21st birthday, 19 August 1993. The family didn't tell him until after he'd enjoyed his 21st birthday party three days later so as not to spoil the occasion.

For a couple of weeks after hearing the news Simon went into the depths of depression. Why did Alistair have to die? It just didn't seem fair. Why couldn't he, Simon, have died and not Alistair?

For two or three days at a time he found himself struggling, desperately trying to hold on to his relationship with God, fighting his way through a jungle of anxiety and feelings of self worthlessness, trying to find the peace he once knew.

He became morose, down in the dumps and sat alone in his bedroom. Even at mealtimes, when he'd normally laugh and joke with Deon Briedenhann and his family, whom he lived with in South Africa, he'd sit in silence. He was aware of his own mortality, of the fact that death happens to everyone sooner or later.

But it wasn't long before Simon realised that running away from God wasn't the answer. He missed speaking with God and he made up with his Maker, despite the way he felt.

Now once more Simon was feeling down in the dumps, this time because his one and only nephew was dead.

After speaking with Vally, one of Deon's workers, Simon arranged to return in the *bakkie* to the Cape, spend Christmas there and decide his next step. Simon had pushed Deon very hard to get the job with Peninsula Poles. They erected masts for lighting and for aerials. Some of the masts which were used for mobile phone networks were 53 metres high. His job was a temporary one, holding the purse strings and keeping a record of who was employed on what particular days. Vally worked full time for Deon; all the others who worked on this job were casual labourers paid by the day.

Before Simon and Vally could go back to Cape Town, there was a back tyre on the *bakkie* to fix. In the end it meant replacing the tyre.

The next day, Wednesday 15 December, the two of them were well on their way on the 800-mile journey home. Simon got on well with Vally, who acted as co-driver as they zoomed along the freeway.

Simon began to open up to Vally about all the tragic news he'd heard recently—his grandmother's death, the tragic death of Alistair back in the summer, then little Timothy's still birth.

'You know something, Vally? I'm not afraid to die,' he said as he drove along. 'You see, if I die I know I'll go straight to heaven.'

Vally grunted something, then drifted off into sleep again.

In the peace that followed, Simon sighed deeply. He loved the new emerging South Africa. He loved its people. But he hated the injustice that still remained.

He remembered that tomorrow would be a national holiday when thousands of white Afrikaners would be celebrating their historic victory over the black people at Blood River. If only they could see how stupid racism really was.

5

The Day of the Vow

Tomorrow, the Day of the Vow, sometimes known as Covenant Day, was one of the most important events in the apartheid calendar.

It was on 16 December 1838 that the Afrikaner trekkers gained victory over the Zulu regiments of King Dingaan at Blood River. According to tradition, the few hundred Afrikaners, protected only by their ox wagons, were under siege from 10,000 Zulus. The Afrikaners made a vow before God, promising that if he gave them victory over the black people, they would celebrate the day each year and keep it holy.

The vow was made during the Great Trek in which the Afrikaners travelled further north so they could establish their own Boer republics. Their aim was to get away from the hated British, who disagreed with slavery and abolished it. By being away from the British, the Afrikaners would be answerable only to their God, Jehovah.

Simon knew and loved many Afrikaners. But today's generation was very different from those of long ago. The original Afrikaners saw black Africans as subject people.

Not every Afrikaner was happy with such blatant celebration of racism as the Day of the Vow. Professor Floors van Jaarsveld, a distinguished Afrikaner historian, examined reports of the Afrikaner commander and his clerk and found no mention of such a promise. He went on to show that the covenant in the form it was celebrated was largely the invention of one man on his death bed in 1871.

After attempting to speak on his findings, the professor was tarred and feathered on 28 March 1979. This was an indication of the way some Afrikaners felt about their history. They saw themselves as fighting against the infidel, driven by a Calvinistic ethic to serve God and protect Christian civilisation.

For almost 60 years devout Afrikaners celebrated the Day of the Covenant with a ceremony at the Voortrekker Monument in Pretoria. In recent years it had been commandeered from the National Party by the neo-Nazi Afrikaner Resistance Movement (AWB), who used the ceremony for their own racist aims and displays of paramilitary muscle. Tomorrow, for instance, the AWB leader Eugene Terreblanche was scheduled to give a doom laden speech, calling for his paramilitaries to resist the ANC.

Traditionally, Afrikaners saw themselves as a people of destiny. In their eyes it was a part of their God-given commission to remain separate in every way from the 'heathen' of their new homeland. They permitted no mixing of blood or culture through sexual laxity.

According to the Bible, God cursed Ham. To the early settlers these 'savages' were none other than Ham's descendants. They were ordained by God as servants and slaves to the Afrikaners.

Separate development (known as apartheid) was introduced. Apartheid (pronounced *apart-hate*) was the Afrikaans word for apartness or separation. By the time Simon arrived in South Africa the first time, most of the more obvious signs of apartheid were gone. Whites only beaches, bars and toilets were a thing of the past, or at least there were no racist signs up anymore.

As Simon had grown through his teen years in England he had become acutely aware of the way South Africa was given headline news because of the apartheid system. In his desire to see justice done everywhere, a desire began to develop within him:

South Africa. The two words I've seen so many times on the front covers of magazines and as the headlines of newspapers. The two words I've heard so many times on the news programmes and documentaries. Yet every time I've seen or heard these words they were connected in the same or the next sentence with words like 'apartheid' and 'violence'. Somehow in my mind I couldn't believe this was all there was to those two words.

A burning desire began to grow inside me to go to South Africa and find out for myself what was really going on there. I questioned whether it was as straightforward an injustice as the media made out.

Was there really this much violence in every township? How free was the average black person? How free was the average white person? Could a black person go into a white area and be safe? Was a white person allowed in a black township? Did God have agents in the townships?

So many questions buzz and yet no answer can satisfy me until I see it for myself.

Africa had for centuries lost many young men and women who were seized and transported for the slave trade. Then came the scramble for territory, when Africa was carved up during the 18th and 19th centuries for colonisation and control by the British, French, Portuguese, Germans, Belgians, Spanish and Dutch.

The Dutch first colonised South Africa in 1652, establishing a settlement now known as Cape Town to supply meat, vegetables and water for the Dutch East India Company's fleets on their way to and from the Far East. The settlers gradually moved inland until Cape Colony was formed.

The first Dutch settlers were soon joined by French Huguenots and by some German settlers, who together evolved into a community called the Afrikaners (people of Africa), with their own language Afrikaans. The language developed from Dutch but over time dropped the more complicated rules of Dutch grammar and became distinct from Dutch.

Politically the Afrikaners were the dominant whites who ruled South Africa continuously from the time when the British gave up control in 1910. During the 1948 election the Nationalist Party candidates told voters that apartheid meant 'total segregation'. But by then industries had developed that depended on a stable African workforce. Thus if blacks were expelled completely, this sector of the economy would collapse.

The full force of the resentment the Afrikaners had been holding for generations was turned against the blacks. Many Afrikaners truthfully said, 'We have no quarrel with the blacks, only with the British.' But it was the blacks who felt the lash.

Simon loved to spend time with the black, Coloured and Asian people in the townships of South Africa. He'd hug little black children and sit for hours talking with wizened old Coloured women. Yet many whites even now feared going into the townships, where shootings were commonplace and stabbings happened regularly.

As with many other things, Simon wanted to see things in South Africa for himself before he decided his reaction to them. He wrote after his first visit:

If there's one thing I've learned while being in South Africa it's this: Never judge anybody or any situation until you've spoken to the person or seen the situation for yourself. I'll never watch a news programme again and just decide: 'Oh, that's how it must be.' There's a whole lot of rubbish floating around out there and much of it comes from the twisted mind of the media.

There has been a terrible injustice done in South Africa over the years. I've never met anyone in Britain or South Africa who denies that. There's still injustice in South Africa today. Is there not in Britain? The reason we've all heard so much about South Africa is that they've legalised a particular injustice—racism. Racism is an international problem. It doesn't have 'Made in South Africa' written on it!

By 1987 it was clear that apartheid had failed. Its intention to secure permanent exclusion of black people from power was becoming harder to maintain.

The result was that South Africa's white leader, President P W Botha, who in 1948 had demanded apartheid's immediate and full introduction, by 1987 cautiously led his party in the opposite direction. He agreed that apartheid should be dismantled. But he was held back by the Afrikaner majority among the voters. Every concession made was too little, too late. The widespread impression that white rule was on the slide made it difficult for black leaders to agree to such concessions.

The release from a long prison sentence of Nelson Mandela, deputy leader of the ANC, spelt the beginning of the end for the apartheid system. Step by step, despite setbacks and bloodbaths in the townships, South Africa was inching its way forward to free and fair elections for people of all races on 27 April next year.

Simon, like many other people, was looking forward to the end of celebrating Blood River and the start of the new South Africa, with the justice he'd lived and dreamed for.

6

Ups and downs of family life

Apartheid wasn't the only thing Simon saw as unjust. He grew through his early years acutely aware of injustice in all its many forms. But as a small child the injustice he saw all centred around himself. He'd be deeply hurt if his parents told him off. He'd find it difficult if things didn't go his way. And he hated correction.

His parents encouraged him never to retaliate when people wronged him. They taught him not to be unkind to people who were unkind to him. If people wanted to pick a fight with him, he was encouraged not to fight back.

They later admitted to him that perhaps they'd gone a bit over the top in bringing him up that way.

Simon was being bullied at school. He wrote about one memorable incident in his early teens:

> At school in the dinner hall there are three queues for dinner—two very long queues and a quick service one. In the quick service queue (if you can call it quick) you have to squash up so tightly that you can hardly breathe.
>
> I was in this queue once and my friend, Leon Case, was jammed up tightly behind me. The queue ran alongside a wall and we were about three feet from the food hatch.
>
> Suddenly, some big, well-known bullies came along, trying to push into the queue. They went straight to Leon, who's quite a small boy, and fiercely started pounding him with punches. They were no soft

*punches, either. I could feel the vibrations coming
against my back.*

*Later, when we got outside, I asked Leon how he felt
and said how sorry I was for him being bullied.*

*'What?' he exclaimed. 'I wasn't being bullied. Those
kids were hitting you, not me!'*

'Go on,' I said. 'Pull the other leg.'

*'No, honest,' he argued. 'They were hitting you. I'm
not joking.'*

*I couldn't believe my ears. God must have put an
angel there to shield me from the punches. Leon isn't
the sort of boy who'd lie to me. God was watching
over me.*

The bullying and intimidation didn't come only from
pupils. On one occasion when he was 13 one of the
teachers in a games lesson called him a poof
(homosexual). Simon was furious. When he got home he
discussed the matter with his parents, and his dad offered
to go and see the head of the lower school. The head
took the matter seriously and arranged a meeting
between Simon, his dad and the teacher. Appropriate
apologies were made and the teacher asked forgiveness
of Simon.

Another time about a year later Simon was in the
school sports hall kicking a ball around with a friend
when a teacher shouted at him for being in there. Simon
reckoned that wasn't fair when he was merely having a
sensible game. The teacher, he felt, had shouted at him
abusively.

Simon insisted he wasn't doing anything wrong. That
just annoyed the teacher, who shouted at him even more.
So Simon shouted back at the teacher. When the teacher
told him off strongly for shouting, Simon replied, 'You
treat me like dirt and I'll treat you like dirt. You treat me
with respect and I'll treat you with respect.'

'If you speak to me like that again, I'll take you to the
headteacher.'

'No, you'll take me to the headteacher—*now!*'

With that, they headed off to see the headteacher.
They walked some distance apart. Simon was worried in
case the teacher might hit him.

They told their story to the headteacher, who decided
to call in Simon's dad. In the end the headteacher felt

that, although Simon shouldn't have spoken to the teacher in the way he did, he was quite right to feel the injustice of the situation. It was the teacher himself who was at fault for criticising Simon for being in the sports hall and speaking abusively to him.

When Simon was about 14, he had a growth spurt. He grew a whole foot in one year—at a rate of an inch a month people could almost literally see him growing before their eyes. It was a mega upheaval. Once he asked despairingly, 'Dad, is there any way I can pray and God can stop me growing?'

By the time he'd finished growing he was at least 6ft 7in, though he refused to measure himself after he had reached 6ft 6in.

After that, he often went for walks in the city of Bath. He once said:

I saw some of the guys who used to bully me at school. They were walking down the hill while I was walking up it. They stepped off the pavement into the road, looked up at me and said, 'All right, Si?'

I looked down and said in my deepest voice, 'All right.'

They were the very guys who used to beat me up, and now they were scared of me. Cool!

By now Simon was often depressed and was struggling with the injustices and hypocrisies he saw in the school. The whole future of the school was in question and the staff were in a state of very low morale. This, combined with the negative way he was handled by some of his teachers, meant that at 16 his parents decided to withdraw him from school and allow him to do home schooling as he prepared for his GCSEs.

His parents noticed a leap in Simon's confidence when he was back in the security of home. Unfortunately, his academic ability didn't improve much. He was home schooled with a correspondence course, but he found it tough completing the specified number of study hours on his own. Instead, he spent much of the time daydreaming. Daydreaming had become a necessary release of the pressures he was under.

He got behind with his GCSE work and had to put off taking the exams until the following year. This meant spending two years of studying at home. During this time he was often moody, sulky and difficult to live with.

Simon knew that during most of his teen years he lived a Jekyll & Hyde existence. His friends outside the family saw this ultra-funny person who was the life and soul of every party. They wouldn't have believed that at home he'd be moody, angry with his parents or just sit silently through mealtimes.

Throughout Simon's childhood his dad had told the children Bible stories at breakfast time. The Walls of Jericho had come tumbling down as the children shouted and banged their spoons on the table. They'd make pictures of Bible scenes and stick them in place on a Bible 'time line' that Barbie had made and stuck up around the dining room.

As a teenager, Simon gave the impression of finding these times boring. But his parents carried on regardless, and it paid off in the end. Simon came to life when they told or read stories of famous Christians such as Fred Lemon, the convict turned Christian, and Brother Andrew, God's smuggler. Simon began to look at the Bible for himself, going through the whole of Psalms and underlining what God is like.

Whenever Simon was reminded of God's call on his life and the promises from God that had been brought into his life his whole face would light up. Mark and Melanie Brooks, leader of the young teens in the church, said they'd never known anyone respond so well to encouragement. Barbie would tell teachers to try a bit of encouragement. They'd come back and say, 'Thanks for the tip. It really works.'

Later, when Simon was 18, he went back to work in his infant school as a voluntary helper. He had a way with little children. They'd feel safe and secure with him. When Mark and Melanie Brooks' son, Daniel, was three Simon would get him to jump off the kitchen table and then catch him. Simon would also hold him upside down by his feet, much to the delight of little Daniel and the horror of his parents.

Simon never thought about clearing up a mess after him. It drove the rest of the family absolutely crazy. They were expected to do things for him.

He enjoyed seeing his brothers and sisters get really wound up. He'd drop litter in the street or throw chocolate wrappers out of the window on purpose. That was sure to evoke a reaction.

'Pick that litter up, Simon.'

'No, it gives someone a job.'

He'd be deliberately provocative about 'women's work', too.

The once innocent relationship Simon had with his big sister Sarah turned into a fight for survival. For the six years of his life from the age of 10 to 16 their relationship was extremely stormy. At one point after a furious argument Sarah genuinely thought he'd come into her room in the middle of the night to kill her.

Apologies never came easily with Simon. Sarah told him she felt she was always making apologies to him but he wasn't returning them. After that, he'd think things through, then knock on her door and stand there with a sheepish grin. 'I'm sorry, Sarah,' he'd say.

Simon would never let Sarah go up or down the stairs first. She even feared that one day he might push her down the stairs.

Until Simon was 14, he and Sarah were roughly the same height. Then he started to get stronger and the fights had to stop. He'd play his music very loudly, leaving his door open to make things much worse. It was a deliberate ploy to be annoying to Sarah and the rest of the family.

When Simon was about 15 and Mum and Dad were away, he and Sarah each had a friend to stay. At about three o'clock in the morning they couldn't sleep and were bored so they all trundled off to the nearest park, a five-minute walk away. They sat on the swings and generally messed around, but then concluded it wasn't adventurous enough.

They came back home and decided to go exploring. The next-door neighbour had recently died and his huge old house was deserted. They decided it'd be great fun to climb up the scaffolding and in through the window. The only problem was they reckoned there was some kind of evil presence in the house. They didn't know whether it'd be a good idea to do it.

For over an hour they debated about it, worried about going into a place where Satan was in control. Their two friends, not having much understanding of the Bible, were a bit baffled by their discussion of this. They prayed about it and decided it wasn't such a good idea, so they called off the plan and went to bed.

Not long after that, Simon had a dream of this huge box like a trunk opening slowly. There was a light coming out and there seemed to be a ghost inside. After that dream, both Simon and Sarah were grateful they hadn't broken into the house.

When Sarah was 17 she started going out with Dave, who later became her husband. Simon, then 16, was very hurt that she hadn't told him about Dave. He decided to be mean and began to spread rumours about what they were getting up to together.

This persuaded Sarah to sit down with Simon and his brother Daniel and tell them about her boyfriend. From then on Simon and Sarah's relationship was completely different. Simon spoke with Sarah and Dave for hours and hours about all kinds of things—swearing, sex, the end of the world and a host of other fascinating subjects. In keeping with their belief in waiting until marriage before having sex, they were very strict about their relationship. Simon watched them with keen interest and began to absorb some of their moral views.

By now Simon was learning not to take himself too seriously. His mum's wonderful sense of humour had rubbed off on to him.

From as far back as Simon could remember, Barbie had played fun tricks on the children each April Fool's Day. When he was six, his mum sewed up the shirt sleeves of the children's school uniforms, telling them all to hurry up and get ready for school. After they struggled for a few minutes, she told them it was a joke. Simon loved it.

The following year, she turned the table upside down, took the chairs away and set breakfast on the underside of the table. Simon and the other children had a memorable breakfast sitting cross-legged on the dining room floor.

Another year, Barbie got up early and made breakfast.

'What's for breakfast?' Simon asked when he came downstairs.

'Spaghetti bolognese.'

'*What?* We don't have spaghetti for breakfast, do we?' he asked.

'Of course we do.'

Simon went purple with rage and stormed upstairs to his dad.

'Daddy, I *won't* eat spaghetti bolognese for breakfast!'

Peter replied: 'If Mummy's made it, you need to eat it.'

Simon stamped downstairs again.

'April Fool, Simon!'

After that, his face lit up and he had two helpings of the most unusual breakfast ever.

Another time Barbie put all the clocks forward by 15 minutes and sent the children off early to school. When their friends came to collect them at the usual time, she told them the Reynolds children had already left and they'd better run to school.

Barbie got her come-uppance one April when she came downstairs to find that Simon and the others had totally transformed the sitting room. The pictures were upside down, all the furniture had been moved around and nothing was the same as it had been. Simon had at long last got his own back.

As a young adult he was becoming a master of fun. One time he, Dave and some of the others were down at the Abbey Courtyard in Bath for New Year's Eve. Simon was pretending to be drunk, though he hadn't had a drop of alcohol. On the stroke of midnight he rushed about, flinging his arms around everyone he could see—even the men and the boys—and giving them huge great kisses! He saw a man and woman rolling around cuddling on the floor near the abbey doors. He leapt on them and joined in the cuddling. Dave thought it was hilarious.

Dave went with Simon to London for another New Year's Eve. They were near Big Ben. Simon was stopping traffic on Westminster Bridge, leaning into cars and giving people hugs.

In contrast to his grandpa's comments about young Simon's hesitation on the diving board, Simon as a teenager had learned to jump in with both feet. He remembered Dave asking for Simon's help in laying a lawn at his house. Between them they moved three and a half tons of soil. The only way to flatten it down was to put a one-metre square wooden board on the soil and jump on it. Simon was jumping on these boards with his size 13 boots making a terrible racket. The whole neighbourhood knew what was going on.

While Sarah was in the USA for a year Simon wrote regularly to her. When he was away himself, he wrote to each individual in the family and he generally remembered birthdays.

Daniel and Simon were close in age but very different in personality. They had a good relationship but it was stormy at times.

When Simon was 12 he and Daniel shared a room and Simon remembered talking about girls, sex and other issues that were a bit over Daniel's head at the time. He always wanted answers to his questions. He'd pick a subject like masturbation and discuss it at great length. Daniel being only 10 didn't have a clue what he was on about but carried on the discussion anyway.

Then Simon talked the subject of masturbation through with his dad and came back to Daniel with a report on the subject.

The two boys would sometimes talk till one or two in the morning. Daniel. the younger of the two, would be just getting off to sleep when Simon would say, 'Daniel! Daniel!'

'Yeah.'

'There's just one other thing I wanted to say . . .'

As a young teenager Simon kept a little red book with the names of each bird he and Daniel had shot and killed. They'd go out with an air rifle, travel by a bus and walk through the woods shooting anything that moved— sparrows, crows, even squirrels. Once they were chased off by the farmer. Another time Simon shot a beautiful big duck. Feathers were flying everywhere as this poor, wounded duck struggled down to the water.

Simon flinched as he remembered how cruel teenagers could be at times.

One time at school Daniel was beaten up by a bully. Daniel told him, 'I'll get my big brother on to you.'

'Yeah, yeah, I believe you,' the lad replied.

'OK, I'll meet you in the park after lunch.'

Simon was doing home schooling at the time and Daniel asked for his help at lunchtime. Together Simon and Daniel went to the park.

'OK, what's your problem?' Simon asked menacingly, towering over the lad.

'Oh, er, nothing.'

With that Simon picked up the lad by the scruff of the neck and said, 'Leave him alone from now on.'

Although Simon terrified the lad, he didn't frighten his brothers and sisters. They knew, like he did, what a big softie he was deep down.

Simon was clear where he stood on issues and was always firm about them. Daniel went through a very carefree stage and that annoyed Simon. He found it hard that Daniel was away from God and yet seemed to be having a good time.

Once, Daniel bought a little old Honda 70 motorbike for next to nothing that didn't work. He and Simon fixed it up. Simon drove round their garden with no helmet, carrying any little kids who dared climb on board.

Another motorbike Daniel bought didn't even have an engine. The two of them once pushed it to the top of their road. Simon got on the front and Daniel on the back and they coasted all the way down into Bath city centre. Then they pushed it all the way up the long, long hill to their house.

On the dance floor, Simon always refused to dance conventionally. Instead, he acted the buffoon, getting the attention of the whole dance floor as a result.

Unlike Daniel, he wasn't bothered about money. 'What would I do with lots of money?' he asked Daniel once. He preferred to walk than to buy cars. Sometimes he walked eight miles to work rather than catch the bus. Possessions didn't mean a thing to him.

The one exception was his collection of music tapes. He loved heavy rock, African and South American music, classical and Christian rock. He was very conscious of the spirit behind the music. He was against satanic music (including music by groups such as Black Sabbath) and backward subliminal messages. He listened to the lyrics and rejected anything with messages that he considered inappropriate.

On the other hand, he wanted to talk through anything controversial. He would ask Daniel's and everyone's views on the subject. Typical of many teenagers, he sought to formulate his thinking by arguing against every view.

When Simon mowed the lawn, if any plant was in the way he'd kill it. The family had a weeping willow and one day when he was tidying up the garden he got the shears and lopped the whole lot off. It made it so much easier to cut the grass! The willow never grew the same again.

Daniel enjoyed keeping ducks and chickens, eventually selling the eggs for a profit. Simon wasn't interested in poultry. He'd say, 'One of your chickens has just *done* an egg, Daniel.' Once, when Daniel went away to India with his parents, Simon agreed to look after the ducks and chickens.

When Daniel got back, Simon met him at Heathrow Airport with some sad news. He said in his deep voice, 'By the way, Daniel. I'm sorry, I shot your cockerel.'

Simon had forgotten to shut the ducks away for the night. The fox had come and disturbed them. Simon had to shoot Daniel's air rifle to frighten the fox, then round up all the ducks and shut them away.

He was really cross with all those ducks—he didn't like them anyway—and had just got back to sleep when the cockerel started crowing. Furious at more disturbance, Simon took the air rifle, marched down the garden to the coop clad only in a pair of garish yellow boxer shorts, and shot its head off as it stuck its head almost down the gun barrel out of curiosity.

For weeks afterwards the neighbours couldn't understand why the cockerel wasn't crowing anymore. No one in the family had the courage to tell them Simon had shot it.

Simon and Daniel had a big fist fight once. Daniel wanted to use the phone but Simon wouldn't let him. He *had* to speak to his girlfriend when she called. It was a matter of life or death, of course.

Defiantly, Daniel went upstairs to use the extension, which was a cordless phone. Daniel heard Simon coming upstairs so he ran into the bathroom and locked the door behind him.

Simon started banging on the door. 'Daniel! I told you not to use the phone.' He then invoked the five-minute rule. In the Reynolds family anyone could give a five-minute warning of wanting to use the phone. The person on the phone had to wind up the conversation and, if necessary, call back later.

The banging on the door increased, with Daniel taunting him because he couldn't get in. Eventually when Daniel had finished talking, he opened the door and Simon snatched the phone off him.

'Just 'cos you're big you can't push me around,' Daniel said.

With that, Simon grabbed his younger brother and pushed him backwards into the bathroom. With nowhere to go, Daniel stepped back into the bath. There was a window behind the bath. Simon pushed Daniel even harder and he went right through the window—two floors up! Fortunately, his head hit the middle crossbar and only his back went through the pane itself.

Daniel used the force of his head hitting the crossbar to jump forward and catch Simon directly in the face. Simon started laying into Daniel until his dad, Peter, managed to frog-march Simon away. Although his dad was a mere six feet tall, Simon knew when he was beaten. He had always had a healthy respect for his parents.

Simon's clothes were an embarrassment to his younger brother Daniel. Simon wasn't bothered about fashion. In fact, he was anti-fashion. His mum Barbie found the state of his clothes embarrassing, too. But Simon didn't care what he wore.

When he lived at home, Simon used to eat whatever was in the fridge. The next family meal would be in the fridge and he'd have the whole lot for himself. He'd open the fridge, get a bottle of milk out, lean one arm on the open door and drink the whole bottle in one go. If Daniel did the same thing Simon would grass on him. His mum finally decided to buy Simon a whole pint of milk for himself each day, but he still managed to clear the fridge of milk.

They'd have furious rows about milk. 'I don't drink more than one pint a day,' Simon would declare.

'Yes, you do. You know you do.'

He'd be absolutely convinced he was right. But as soon as he went to South Africa the family suddenly found they had loads of extra milk! They'd laughed with him over the phone about that.

When Susie was very little Simon used to play with her a lot. He loved little children and babies. But as a young teenager he found Susie a pain. He was always grumpy and would step on her toes when he was going up or down stairs. When she was 15 or 16 they became really close again. He knew now that he was Susie's best friend.

Simon returned from South Africa the first time a changed person as far as Susie and the rest of the family were concerned. He was polite, cleared the table and said 'Please' and 'Thank you'.

Once Susie came round to Simon's house for the evening and they ended up talking. Although he was supposed to go to evening class in Bristol, he said he found their conversation far more interesting.

He asked her, 'Have you ever driven a car?'

'No, never.'

'Well, you can have a go now.'

He drove their parents' car to a college just outside Bath and she took over, driving up and down fields and lanes within the college grounds. After that they sat and talked together in the garden. From then on he often let Susie drive the car on private land. When she turned 17 her dad was surprised at how well she could drive.

Simon and his best friend James would go round to see Susie when she was in the sixth form. One time she'd waited for them during lunchtime and when they didn't show up she went to her lesson. Halfway through the lesson she had a message that there were two people to see her. She got permission to leave the lesson, went out and met up with Simon and James and chatted for a while.

Eventually the teacher came looking for her and was extremely annoyed to find her talking with these two strange young men.

Simon took the teacher to one side and said, 'Look, it's family business. We'll just be another five minutes.'

'Oh, I'm very sorry,' she said. 'Do carry on. Take your time.'

Simon could get round people without actually lying. It was one attribute that Susie claimed she got from Simon.

Simon and Susie had many similarities. Like other teenagers Simon found his parents difficult; so did she. Simon understood how she felt and their relationship became much closer. They also shared the same enthusiasm for working in South Africa.

Susie could never understand Simon's line of thinking on boy/girl relationships. He'd have a particular female friend and they'd like each other, but he objected to the title 'going out'.

Simon and Susie often went rowing up the river and had long talks about God, relationships, the family and where each of them was going in life.

Joff, Simon's youngest brother, was very special to Simon. Joff brought out the soft side in him. His parents noticed that Joff melted Simon's often hard exterior.

Simon remembered when Joff was still a toddler the Reynolds kids pretending to be the Famous Five, switching off all the lights in the house. Joff was so little he only qualified for being the dog in the Enid Blyton stories they acted out.

As Simon grew into his early teens he'd often mess around with Joff, picking him up, swinging him around with one hand, lifting him high in the air or pushing him up against the wall and letting him drop on to the radiator. He'd also throw Joff around on the settees. Joff found it lots of fun, though grown-ups tended to get upset about the rough way Simon seemed to handle him.

Later, though, when he was in a bad mood Simon would tend to boss Joff around. He'd come in and turn over the TV while Joff was watching a particular programme.

Simon often would hire out a '15' video and watch it with his friends. Joff was too young to be allowed to watch it. He'd hang round outside and periodically rattle the door. This tended to wind Simon up and he'd chase Joff up the stairs threatening what he'd do to him after his friends had left.

Sometimes Simon bribed his kid brother Joff into buying a Mars bar or something similar from the shop five minutes' walk down the road. 'You can have a 5p chew if you get it for me,' he'd say tantalisingly. Joff thought it was really worth it.

Simon's relationship with Joff took on a new dimension after he left home. He'd take Joff out for a drive and buy him loads of sweets, or Joff would come round to his flat and they'd watch a video. They had lots of fun trying to cook a meal together. Simon grew up convincing himself that cooking was 'women's work'. Now as an adult he was having to develop a new skill—even learning things from his kid brother and returning home for a weekly cooking lesson with his mum.

Once, Simon took 12-year-old Joff to an empty park-and-ride car park and taught him how to drive. Another time at a Bible Week, he took Joff and a couple of his friends in the car and got into two-wheel skids on the grassy slopes by using the handbrake.

Yes, Simon loved his family even though he'd been an awkward teenager. And he knew they liked his crazy ways. He was brilliant at mimicking the rest of his family. He had a wild laugh and would let rip whenever he thought something was really funny.

He often felt guilty and discouraged about the way he'd treated his family. Then his mum wrote him that letter.

7

Together again

Simon remembered how he'd been very awkward while he was in his mid-teens. He challenged his parents' attitudes and beliefs, scorned his brothers and sisters and was sulky and moody. At times, he knew, his parents despaired of him.

But his obstinacy hadn't started in his teen years. Even as a small child he was often questioning authority, never content to accept the status quo.

He knew how his childhood had caused his parents a lot of anguish. Big sister Sarah was compliant almost from birth. If as a toddler she crawled towards the grate of their Rayburn coal fire they'd tell her, 'No!' She'd then put her hand out to touch the grate. His parents would tap her hand and she'd be upset and never do it again.

'We thought we had this side of things sorted out, but Simon was a different kettle of fish,' recalled his dad once. 'He was physically well developed long before any child we've ever come across. I remember he'd crawl across the room to the large rubber plant and he'd manage to reach up and pull it over. We'd put the plant back and he'd do it again. At that stage of development we expected him to learn, but he didn't. It went beyond the toddler years. We wondered if we were being too hard on him.

'We had a formula that worked well with Sarah but not with Simon. Were we being too restrictive or too harsh? We tried to adjust, but then we became too lenient. We really struggled to handle him without being too repressive and yet remain firm.

'Daniel, his younger brother, was much more in line with his older sister—contented, happy, responsive, always wanting to please. Simon, on the other hand, wanted to challenge the direction or correction that was brought.'

In bringing Simon up, Peter and Barbie Reynolds later told him they tried to give two positives for each negative. They'd have to go round looking for something to praise him for. Barbie at times had to set something up just so she'd be able to say something positive to him each day.

He was very strong willed and he often contested. They had to admit: 'We're struggling because we've never had to bring up a son before.'

As a teenager, Simon was obstinate and he knew his attitude in the home was dreadful, so much so that his parents at times despaired of him.

By then the fact that he lived in a family of committed Christians was in his view a disadvantage. He said at the time that he wished he didn't live in a Christian family because it was so difficult to be good. He saw his older sister as good while by comparison he was bad.

But even that wasn't new. At the age of four, he once said, 'Mummy, if I be baptised will I always be good?' He had a picture of himself even then as being not good.

The arguments between Simon and his parents grew more and more heated. One time, when Simon was in his mid-teens, Peter said to him, 'If you feel I'm wronging you, instead of burying it deep down, why don't you do what Jesus said and bring another Christian in who can give an impartial judgment?'

Each time, Simon shrugged off the suggestion. Eventually Peter reached the point of frustration.

'I'm not happy to leave it unresolved,' he said to Simon one day. 'I'm calling in Paul Wakely.'

Simon was annoyed with his dad but reluctantly agreed to give it a try. Paul Wakely was one of the leaders of the church Simon attended. Paul came and sat in on the discussion and then, as predicted, brought an impartial judgment. He pointed out where Simon was wrong and also showed where Peter needed to make changes. Neither of them felt humiliated or in any other way put down.

Eventually, in July 1990, Simon and his parents had a heart to heart session. His mum wrote him a letter afterwards, a letter that he now treasured:

As I've pondered and considered the things you shared with us last night—and thank you for sharing them, even though it cost you—I've felt that I wanted to write you a letter. I think I can share my heart better in a letter on this occasion than if I tried to tell you.

I've looked through the albums and thought back to the time when you were a little baby. I remember the deep joy I knew when you were born. I was so thrilled to have a boy. You were a very easy baby, always hungry and full of energy. The first occasion we ever took a picture of you there was a determined look in your eye. Whenever you set your mind on anything you went for it.

Simon, being sandwiched between an older sister and an easy-going younger brother has never been easy for you, because you are so different by nature and character. You've always been a thinker, taking things to heart in a much deeper way than the others.

When you were three I wrote this in my baby record book about you: 'Simon doesn't find discipline easy to take. But as we train him up according to his own way, the way that God has purposed for him, then Simon is going to come forth as gold. He will be strong as a rock, ready to take the knocks that the call of God upon his life is going to bring.'

We didn't always get it right. Looking back, I think perhaps we overdisciplined you because we didn't understand what was going on inside you. But of one thing I'm deeply grateful: God will turn our failure and mistakes to his own purposes in your life because he loves you.

When I think of you as a young boy I remember your wonderful smile and your warm, twinkling eyes. I remember your extraordinary sensitivity to the feelings of others. You were able to empathise and really care in a way that was unusually sensitive for a small boy.

As you came into your teens you certainly did have your struggles. You had difficulties at school, which were often misjudged by teachers and staff because few had the time or opportunity to get to know you. But those who did were impressed by what they saw. One of them, Mr Scott, said it was a shame that others didn't have 'the privilege of seeing the side of Simon I've seen'.

Then you opted to do your GCSEs at home, which turned out to be a hard slog. But you kept at it and finished the exams. Well done!

Outside the home you're talkative, caring, sensitive and much used by God. In the home you're just the opposite. You've struggled with this for years and we've watched, wishing we could help, but finding that no matter how we try we only seem to make it worse.

I remember from my teen years what it was like to have my own relationship with God. I found it very difficult to share that with my parents. It seems to be a part of growing up and establishing a relationship with God that is totally independent of one's parents. Also I believe there's an unseen pressure on Christian leaders' kids to conform. But we don't want you to conform, Simon.

God has called you for himself, not for our benefit. He is moulding and shaping you through all the things you've been through for the very unique path he has planned for you. You're not just anybody. God has chosen you to be a servant and Jesus said: 'The servant is the greatest of all.' As you walk humbly with him, he is going to open doors for you that at the moment you can't imagine possible.

You mentioned your dread of coming back to visit us when you're married and your children hearing what you were like as a child. I look forward to it, Simon! I look forward to telling them what an adventurous and strong little boy you were, and showing them pictures of your wonderful smile. I'll tell them how caring you've always been of people who were hurting or in difficulty. They won't be surprised because that's the kind of daddy they'll know.

But I won't be surprised if you don't have one child at least who will be amazed but also relieved to hear that you were naughty and had to be disciplined often for bad attitudes. It will give them hope because they'll see how you turned out and they'll be encouraged that there's hope for them, too. After all, your own dad wasn't such an angel in his teens. Even in some of his photos his attitude stinks.

God's grace is an amazing thing. We don't deserve it, but he pours out his love upon us and his Spirit transforms us as we walk closely with him. Day by day, *little by little, crisis after crisis he changes us to be more like Jesus.*

In just three weeks you'll be 18, an adult in your own right. I believe that as you leave home and go to South Africa many changes will take place. You will grow (not physically, I hope) in leaps and bounds. You'll be stretched and broadened in your outlook and understanding of many things. You'll be exposed to new experiences, some of them very good and enjoyable, others shocking and upsetting to you. You'll experience feelings and emotions you've not had before. You'll grow in your understanding of people, and God himself will teach you his ways—if you stay close to him.

Of one thing I want you to be certain: In spite of all the difficulties we've had as you've grown up, we love you with all our hearts. We count it a privilege to have you in our family, 'cos there's no one else like you. I for one am a very proud mum.

On New Year's Day 1991 Simon wrote to his parents from South Africa:

This is a long overdue letter that I've put off and put off, yet deep down I know I really want to write it.

Since coming to South Africa I've stayed with many different kinds of people from various backgrounds and walks of life. Everything from mud huts to luxurious country estates, from the very rich to the very poor. In seeing these lifestyles I've been able to have just a taste of some of the different paths of life people are living.

In all this, through the tough times and the easy times, I miss home very much. I miss sitting around the meal table and hearing everyone talk. I miss being able to tell you 'what happened to me today'. I miss the constant ringing of the telephone and Dad saying: 'Are you free to answer that?' I even miss the little squabbles Joff and Susie have.

While being here I've thought about home a lot. I've also had time to think about my life, my future, my past, my relationship with God and my relationship with you. Concerning my relationship with you, I think the bottom line is—I messed up.

When I think back to disputes that came up at home, I can remember times when I thought you were very fair and others when I thought you were unfair. But no matter what I've said, I've known you've got this parenting thing pretty well sussed. You actually do an unbelievably good job at it.

In exactly the same way in marriage, I've never met any couple anywhere with a better, stronger relationship than you two. And that makes me proud. You're my parents.

Looking back on incidents that got blown up between you and me, although I would never have acknowledged it at the time, it wasn't who was right or wrong that was the problem; it was the heart attitude in me. The Bible says: 'From the heart man speaks.' Because of the condition of my heart, the words I spoke when I was upset were hurtful and harmful and certainly unwarranted.

Many students and people who'd left home told me: 'When you leave home and then come back, all the problems seem to have straightened themselves out.'

I thought and prayed about it and then God showed me something. When I come home, things aren't going to automatically straighten out. If the problem's in my heart I'll bring it home with me. It needs to be defeated and left out here.

Many ask how you brought us up on certain issues so I can advise them! I love talking about you. I feel so proud saying, 'I don't know anybody with greater integrity than my dad,' and: 'I can hardly believe how my mum's able to show her love to us like nobody else can when she must be least feeling like it.'

I love you two so much. I'm just so proud to have you as my mum and dad. After the way I've treated you and behaved, I don't deserve the love and care you've shown back to me. Despite what I've ever said, you've been the best parents I could have hoped for. Yet sometimes I've behaved like the most ungrateful, unappreciative son a parent could ever dream of.

Please forgive me for my attitude and for the hurtful and harmful things I've said in the past. I'm really, really sorry for the pain and grief I've put you through.

I'm not writing off my childhood and adolescent years as a failure in terms of my relationship with you.

I see it as a training period for my future. I just messed up a lot, that's all. The devil might have won a few battles but I'm definitely going to win the war.
With my love for ever,
Simon

When Simon wrote his letter, his younger brother Daniel was going through a rebellious stage. He commented:

God's manipulating Daniel's little joyride through a training course that later is gonna make him one tough cookie for the devil to try anything on, just like I am.

As it turned out, Simon was right. Daniel later found his way back to God and became 'one tough cookie for the devil to try anything on'.

Looking back, Simon's parents recalled how they knew of many families where things had reached a crunch point and the parents had said to their teenagers, 'You're out!' The result was that their children continued in rebellion and rejection of God.

Peter wrote a letter to Daniel expressing how he felt and saying that at this point parents often throw their teenagers out. But Peter said, 'Whatever happens, I never want to sever our friendship.' Daniel was cross about the letter but took it to the USA and read it again and again.

Daniel's lifestyle was both a frustration and a sorrow. But the important thing was to keep the relationship going.

From their difficult experience of Simon and later of his brother Daniel, Peter and Barbie would tell delegates at their Marriage and Family seminars, 'Don't ever lose hope. And never reject your teenager simply because he or she is difficult at times.'

For parents who were despairing of their teenage children, Barbie would say simply, 'Hang in there. Focus on the good things and keep on loving them.'

'Be consistent,' Peter would say. 'Do justice, love mercy, walk humbly. Apply the same rules to yourself as you do to your children. Show patience. Honour your teenager, give weight to him or her. Respect your teenager, attribute honour even if it's rebuffed.

'Keep loving them. You'll reap what you sow. Love never fails.'

8

A sudden stop

With his co-driver, Vally, fast asleep, Simon had time to be himself. He switched on one of his many music tapes and grooved away to the rock music. He loved music of most kinds, but especially rock and heavy metal. Music was one of his greatest interests, and he had a huge collection of tapes.

Not only did he enjoy listening to music; he enjoyed playing it as well. His parents had encouraged him when his infant teacher pointed out a natural talent in music. Although they couldn't afford a flute at the time, the family prayed together until they had enough money to get one.

Peter and Barbie felt it was important to nurture each of their children's unique interests. They wanted Simon to discover for himself his own gifts and talents.

Their many years of encouraging him to practice paid off later. Simon's skills on the flute were well known to the church and to most of his friends. He'd never been particularly interested in studying music formally or in getting grades, though he took lessons until he was 18. He enjoyed the flute simply for the pleasure it brought him. He'd join with the other church musicians to play beautiful worship songs in church meetings.

Back in Bath he'd been one of the church musicians. Even out here in South Africa he'd often been asked to play a solo in church or to join other musicians in using his flute to express his love for God.

People sometimes thought it strange that this giant of a man could play such a delicate instrument. In many ways, though, the flute was an ideal instrument for reflecting various moods. The top notes were bright and clear, the lower notes softer and less penetrating. The instrument lent itself to bright cheerful tunes, especially ones that jumped about a lot. By complete contrast, Simon could play slower, more lyrical tunes, with a kind of melancholy and seriousness.

The way he shaped his lips was called the *embouchure.* Fortunately for Simon, an accident when he was nine helped him to improve his *embouchure* and make him a better flautist. He and his family were on a walk with their friends Steve and Helen Appel and their three children.

In a football tackle, young Simon fell on the road. He landed face down and by sheer chance caught his lip on the back of Steve's wellington boot. Blood poured everywhere and it was soon obvious that he'd have to go to the casualty department at the local hospital.

The result was that he had to have three stitches. When they were taken out a few days later, he ended up with a permanent fat lip.

At first Simon worried that he'd never be able to play the flute again. But once his lip had healed completely he found his *embouchure* had improved immensely.

Back in the cab of the *bakkie,* Simon was listening to the music and enjoying the relaxation of driving along a quiet highway in the South African countryside. He'd always loved driving, almost as much as he enjoyed walking. He drove fast whenever he could. Someone in England once described him as an adrenaline junky. The truth was, he might drive fast at times but at least he was a safe driver.

Driving conditions in South Africa weren't quite the same as in England. The cross-country roads here were very different from the motorways in much of England. Most were two-lane highways with rough dirt breakdown lanes either side. In the townships the roads deteriorated into dirt roads that became mud tracks after a rainstorm.

It was now 11.00 in the morning and Simon and Vally were an hour away from Cape Town and neighbouring Somerset West. Ahead, Simon saw a car travelling at a reasonable speed but not quite fast enough for Simon—who was keeping a steady 110 kilometres per hour all the way.

As Simon's *bakkie* drew closer, the car in front pulled over to the left on to the dirt shoulder to make it easier for him to overtake. There's a custom in South Africa that when someone overtakes, as a courtesy the one in front pulls on to the dirt shoulder to let the other vehicle get by. Although it's technically against the law, it's something almost everyone does.

Simon overtook the car on the right, then put on his hazard warning lights in the customary way to thank the driver for letting him pass. He then pulled away from the car along this straight stretch of road.

And then it happened.

The new tyre Simon had had fitted on to the offside back wheel yesterday burst with an explosion and the *bakkie* suddenly took on a mind of its own. Instinctively, Simon hit the brakes with all his force and his knuckles whitened as he gripped the steering wheel to bring the *bakkie* back under control.

But even with all his might Simon couldn't stop the *bakkie* veering towards the centre of the road.

With a surge of strength, Simon yanked the steering wheel down, at the last split second pulling the *bakkie* back to the left. Inevitably, with no rubber left on the rear wheel, the *bakkie* collided with the crash barrier on the left-hand side of the road and spun around.

Simon felt the seatbelt grip tightly around his body as the *bakkie* hit the small crash barrier on the side of the dirt shoulder. The force of the impact bounced the *bakkie* out into the road again and before Simon knew what was happening, it went into a complete 360-degree spin, coming to rest on the dirt shoulder once again.

There was an eerie silence as Simon realised how close he'd come to death. He knew he'd been injured—his right leg hurt worse than he'd ever known. But at least he was alive. As he sat there wondering what to do next, a neatly dressed man appeared outside the cab.

'You all right, son?' he asked.

'Yeah, I think so,' Simon replied briefly.

'Hi. I'm the guy you just overtook back there.'

José de Fratus was a sales rep used to travelling along this route. The accident had taken him completely by surprise. A few moments after Simon had overtaken, José suddenly saw up ahead black bits of rubber flying everywhere. As he drew up near the *bakkie* he noticed that the back tyre on the right had completely disintegrated. The cab of the *bakkie* didn't appear to be badly damaged. Simon was sitting there looking dazed.

'Please don't move me,' said Simon. 'My legs are hurting like crazy.'

'OK,' said José. 'I'll get some help as soon as I can. Anything else I can do for you?'

'Yeah, could you please contact Deon Briedenhann and tell him what's happened? I'll give you the number.'

José promised to tell Deon the situation as soon as he got to a phone. He then managed to flag down a passing car and ask the driver to call in at Piketberg, a small town 15 minutes down the road. He knew the town had a cottage hospital and an ambulance.

José waited with Simon until the ambulance came. He noticed that Simon was bleeding from his mouth. When he knew that Simon was in good hands he went on his way so that he wouldn't be too late for his next appointment.

Neither of the ambulancemen knew much English. Simon kept pointing to his leg and wincing with the pain, and a look of understanding came over them. They also touched his arm and he realised that it, too, was probably broken.

As quickly as they'd appeared, the ambulancemen suddenly disappeared. Simon could hear them talking loudly and unloading various bits of equipment from the ambulance.

Then it struck him. Where was Vally? Last seen he'd been sleeping like a baby beside Simon in the cab of the *bakkie*. What had happened to him?

Unknown to Simon, Vally was lying on the dirt shoulder. Unlike Simon, he hadn't put on his seatbelt. The force of the impact had propelled him through the passenger door. The ambulancemen saw that Simon was fully coherent and were much more concerned for Vally, who was obviously in a lot of pain.

There was nothing for it but to wait and think. Simon didn't mind Vally being sorted out first. It was to make friends with people like Vally that Simon had come to South Africa the first time round. That was when he was good at keeping a daily diary.

9

Diary of an 18-year-old

Tuesday 25 September 1990

Arrived in Durban 10.40 am. I was picked up by a guy called Al, who took me back to his place for coffee. Then we went to Peter van Niekerk's. Had supper at 6.30 and met Alfias, a black guy who has sort of been adopted by the van Niekerks. Prayed with Peter and Alfias tonight.

Wednesday 26 September

Went into Durban with Peter in the morning. He showed me round the different markets and malls. He also showed me the rough areas to stay away from. Peter's really funny and we have a laugh winding each other up.

I visited Chesterville, one of the most violent townships in the area. On Wednesday 3 October me and Pete Stevens were given the church's minibus, a top-of-the-range luxury traveller, to take a dead body all the way to a church in Harare, Zimbabwe. It took 15 hours with the body on the back seat!

We visited a man who is similar to Benson Idahosa of Nigeria. He's called Prophet Andrew Wutawanashi. You're supposed to address him as 'prophet'. He has a church that has spread throughout Zimbabwe—50,000 strong. He only planted his first church 10 years ago and there were 20 people in it. His church here in Harare where he lives is 2000 strong.

He spent the afternoon with me and Pete and six of his team. Much of the time I was talking with him about signs and wonders. He's done some amazing things. Their church meets on Thursday nights and Sunday mornings. It's a totally black church and they have 100 per cent attendance for both meetings. Tonight we went to the meeting at 7.00 pm. About 1500 people were there at 6.00 pm. An incredible sight!

The meeting finished at 12.15 am, and they say that's normal. At 11.30, I was nearly dropping off when the prophet said my name. He called me up to the front before 2000 people and publicly welcomed me! Then he handed me the mike and asked me to greet the people and encourage them. So I talked for a bit about the church in Bath and how I find the times of meetings here so outrageous. They all laughed.

I talked for about 15 minutes and started to really enjoy it. It was funny having an interpreter, though.

We got home at 1.00 am and, right at the most knackered point of my life, we sat down for a meal.

Saturday 20 October
Hitchhiked down from the border after spending the night on the pavement. Kallie Swart picked us up from Pretoria and took us to Johannesburg.

Sunday 21 October
Went to Kallie Swart's church in Midrand. About 200 there. Went to a lion park in the afternoon. That was excellent!

Tuesday 23 October
Went to supper with Mum's relatives. Quite interesting. It was sticky to start with, but they loosened up later.

Wednesday 24 October
Walked in the afternoon out to Sandton City, to the Mall, three-quarters of an hour's walk. There was a thief running out with some money, but security nailed him good. Drove to Midrand Bible Week in the evening. Helped set up PA until 12.15 am.

Friday 26 October
Went to the leaders' meeting after breakfast. Bryn Jones spoke on apartheid in the church. He was brilliant.

Saturday 27 October
A pastor here called Winston Pienaar is a singer and has recorded four albums. He's just doing his fifth and wants me to come to Cape Town to play my flute for a few songs. Threw a guy in the swimming pool at supper time. The prophet spoke in the evening.

Sunday 28 October

Went to Alan Scotland's seminar on *Christians in Conflict* in the morning, then Keri Jones took the final meeting. We had lunch and then I went back to Dave and Karen Whitewood's. There was a massive thunderstorm tonight, and Dave had to go away on a business conference until Thursday.

Monday 29 October

Went on my own to a township near here called Alexandra. I met two guys there who showed me around. I got loads of pictures.

Tuesday 30 October

Me and Pete sunbathed from 11.00 am to 4.30 pm, in and out of the pool all day. I burned my feet badly. Went to the prayer meeting in the evening and nearly passed out because I think I caught a bit of sunstroke. My feet had really swollen up when I got home so Karen gave me some oil to put on them, which helped.

Wednesday 31 October

I had to rest inside because I think I have sunstroke or something. I can hardly walk, my feet are so sore. They're all red and swollen. Gross! Tomorrow I'm moving into Kallie Swart's house. I'll miss being with the Whitewoods.

Thursday 1 November

In the evening at supper Kallie and Ina tried to talk me into going up to the game reserve, saying that I'd see townships while I'm up there. I called home tonight and Dad said I ought to do whatever Kallie thinks is best. So tomorrow if there's room in the car I'm going. If there's not, I'm staying and will see townships down here in Jo'burg.

Friday 2 November

Went across the road to the church offices where we were picked up by someone called Tracy, who drove us up to a town near Whiteriver. There was room for me in the car—just! A pastor from Whiteriver picked us up there and drove us to the house of another pastor here in Whiteriver. His house is like a hotel! The pastor who picked us up has asked me to preach at his church on Sunday.

Saturday 3 November

We had to wait two hours for this guy to come to take us out for the day. He drove us in a *bakkie*—me in the back and Pete in the front—to a holiday resort up in the mountains. It took an hour and a half to get there 'cos he drove painfully slowly, at 40 km/h! So I asked if I could drive and he agreed. We went to a snake park and saw a giraffe right on the side of the road.

In the evening we went to the church meeting and I had to go up to speak. That was quite cool. There were about 500 people there and the choir did two songs in English they'd been learning especially for us. We left the meeting when the preaching started 'cos it's already put into three languages and one of them isn't English!

Sunday 4 November

My lift didn't arrive to take me to the church I was asked to preach at, so I went to the same one as last night. In the afternoon I drove a *bakkie* out to see some Mozambique refugee camps. They were all mud and straw huts. The living conditions were pretty awful but apparently not as bad as some of the townships.

Friday 9 November

Kallie drove me into Jo'burg to catch the 10 am Greyhound bus to Durban. Dave Phillips met me in Durban when I arrived at 7.00 pm.

Sunday 11 November

Picked up and took to church three mentally disabled people. Had a flat battery in Durban when we stopped for a burger—right in a thunderstorm. We got some guys to push us.

Monday 12 November

Went to Westville Mall to get my photos developed. The car broke down so I had to walk to Jenny's work to tell her. Then I walked up to the van Niekerks to get some stuff. Tracy Haig phoned to say her course was cancelled and we were leaving for Kokstad in 20 minutes. Brad picked me up and we drove first to Pietermaritzberg, then down to Kokstad. We went 220 kph in his BMW 735i!

Tuesday 13 November

Picked up Brandon (7), Brad's son, from school. In the afternoon I looked around the farmyard. A piglet squitted down me when I picked it up. Had a play scrap with Martin (17), Brad's other son.

Wednesday 14 November

Watched a cow give birth in the morning and got some photos. Went to the abattoir and saw sheep, pigs and bulls being slaughtered. In the afternoon I helped Brad clip the bulls' ears with number tags. We did about 100 of them and they kick, fight and buck like crazy.

Saturday 17 November

Went on a game hunt in the evening on the back of a *bakkie*. Using hand-held spotlights we saw buck, rabbits, foxes and wild cats.

Monday 19 November

Went over the border to Transkei with Tracy Haig to see a pastor and his wife, Oliver and Patience. Oliver showed us townships around the area. The whole place was littered with them. Wrote a poem in the afternoon and talked with Martin and Tracy in the evening.

Wednesday 21 November

One of Brad's truck drivers was ill today so I had to drive the truck over into Transkei to deliver meat to two butchers in a place called Kisikisiki, about 2½ hours away. Had a black guy (19) with me. He couldn't speak a word of English, so getting directions out of him was a problem. Had a big pillow-fight with Martin and Tracy in the evening.

Thursday 22 November

Went to the Drakensburg Mountains with Tracy. Climbed up an old river/waterfall full of big rocks. There was a waterfall at the top. We sunbathed by the pool at Sani Pass Hotel. Had to break up a fight where a black guy was beating up his wife. Came home in the evening and listened to music with Martin and Philip (a lodger).

Saturday 24 November

Bought kites for Brandon in the morning and flew one in a field. In the afternoon we made paper darts. Talked with Tracy until 1 am!

Tuesday 27 November

Walked up a hill with Tracy in the morning, just near the farm. From the top you can see vultures and eagles eating the animals that die on the farm. Went to bed early tonight 'cos I was bored.

Thursday 29 November
Left in Brad's six-seater plane at 7 am and got into Durban at 7.45. Went to the church office to meet Dave Phillips and then went to Chesterville township with Sandi Phillips to a Christmas party for pensioners.

Friday 30 November
Walked up to Westville Mall to get my photos and post some letters. When I came back I was locked out, so I had to unscrew the safety bars on a window to break in.

Sunday 2 December
Went to church at 9 am. Dave Phillips spoke. Went back to Roger Owen's for lunch. Everyone was out so I just had to wait for Mark and Avril Bird and their kids to pick me up at 4 pm and take me to their farm in Richmond, near Pietermaritzburg and Durban. I'll be staying here for a week. They have four kids: Douglas (10), Ruth (5), Joanna (3) and Steve (2).

Monday 3 December
Got woken up at 6 am by the kids and had breakfast. Mark said it was too wet to do any work today so we basically did nothing. In the evening I moved my stuff to the house next door, which is empty and owned by Mark and Avril.

Tuesday 4 December
Picked oranges up in the orchard with loads of black women. Drove the truck to the sorting shed to clean and pack the oranges. In the afternoon I mowed the lawn around the farmhouse using the tractor mower.

Wednesday 5 December
Delivered a *bakkie* load of cabbages to a shop in Richmond in the morning. Then went with Mark and two of the kids to a big citrus fruit warehouse about an hour away. Went with two guys in the truck to Ixopo around lunchtime to deliver three tons of oranges. Had raw chicken for lunch. Came back in the afternoon and went to the citrus warehouse with more oranges. Went to bed at 8.30.

Friday 7 December

Went to the orange orchard in the morning to oversee 30 workers picking oranges. Delivered cabbages in the afternoon and worked in the sorting shed for the rest of the day. Got home at 5.30 pm totally knackered and sunburnt.

Saturday 8 December

Had the afternoon free so I sunbathed, had a shower and went shooting with John-Mark. I got stopped by a traffic cop coming back from Richmond for overtaking on some kind of line in the road. He said I could pay R300 now or go to court in January. We had a long chat and he filled out a form I had to sign. After a while he let me off. Very close!

Sunday 9 December

The cows got out in the afternoon so I had to go and chase them back to their field. They got out again in the evening so I had to do the same again.

Monday 10 December

Today I'm in Pietermaritzburg staying with Jeff and Morietta Smart and their daughter Claire (12). Went to church musicians' practice in the evening. They want me to play my flute on Sunday.

Tuesday 11 December

A guy called Des and his friend took me to Hopewell township, where I met and had supper with the pastor, Philemon. He showed me the school he runs and some new toilet cubicles they'd built. A few weeks ago they were using a hole in the ground. In the afternoon we went to Imbali township, which is being rebuilt with proper houses.

Thursday 13 December

In the evening I went to supper with some people in the church. We talked about the end times, demons, weird phenomena—all my favourite subjects!

Friday 14 December

Got picked up at 11.30 am by Rob Spiers, a farmer from Boston. Boston's three quarters of an hour from Pietermaritzburg. He has a wife, Celia, and three kids. I'm staying here at their house tonight.

Saturday 15 December
Another farmer called Mark took me up to a township in the mountains near Boston. There I met Paul and Zonke Sithole. Paul is a black pastor in the township of Umfaga. I went to their farewell/Christmas party for the youth in the afternoon. In the evening we had worms and chicken for supper. I stayed there that night. We heard fighting and then gunshots that evening.

Saturday 22 December
Today was hot and the potatoes were dry enough to pull, so we pulled, sorted, packed and stacked potatoes all day. It was extremely hard work. We started at 7.30 am and worked until 4 pm. I was totally knackered and slept *very* well.

Sunday 23 December
Went to Westville Church in Durban, an outdoor drive-in church in the car park of a mall. It was so hot! After lunch we went to the airport. We flew back to Kokstad in Brad's plane—through a storm.

Tuesday 25 December
Had Christmas dinner on the veranda. It was quite hot. We had cold meats, curry and salad. It would have been too hot for a roast. In the afternoon Tracy and I went to the beach. It was full of people. I rang Mum and Dad in the evening and then went to bed.

Wednesday 26 December
Went for a walk up to the hill where the vultures' nests are. Didn't see any vultures today. In the afternoon I didn't feel too well so I went to bed and just listened to music. In the evening we watched that naff film *Cocoon*. Totally boring.

Thursday 27 December
Went with Tracy and Alex to Sani Pass. It was baking hot today. I sunbathed by the pool while the others went off for a walk. Later I went for a walk by myself to a big waterfall. Got home at about 6.30 and I had a problem breathing. When I breathed deeply I choked. In the evening we watched *Die Hard*.

Friday 28 December
I had a shooting game with Brandon using rubber darts. After lunch Vera drove Alex Hobbs and me to Ixopo

where Avril met us and drove us to Richmond. Alex's brother came to pick her up in the evening and then Mark and Avril and the kids went on holiday. They gave me some boots for Christmas.

Monday 31 December
In the evening I drove the truck (empty) to Pietermaritzburg, about three quarters of an hour away, to a party of some guys I met a while ago. We had a *braai* (barbecue) and then drove into town, picking up anyone who was looking for a party. We had such a laugh! At one party we went to a guy got stabbed. Went to a bar called Legends for 12 o'clock.

Saturday 5 January 1991
Went to Richmond with Mark and drove around looking at black and Indian areas and their differences.

Sunday 13 January
Mark Bird came round today and said God had told him to give me R300. I couldn't believe it! I've been so short of dosh lately and yet felt to give. Now God's giving back. Then Yvonne gave me R60. I'm in a good mood tonight!

Monday 14 January
Went to the airport at 6 am and got a standby ticket for 10 pm. They rushed me through to the plane so I didn't get a chance to call Kobus Swart to tell him what time I was arriving. Arrived in Cape Town at 1.15 am. I decided it was too late to call Kobus so I slept on the airport floor.

Tuesday 15 January
Woke at 4 am with all the noise of another flight coming in. I had to wait until 11 am before anyone came to pick me up. I'm staying with a couple in the church, Neville and Anita Jacobson.

Wednesday 16 January
Spent the day clearing out Ernst's garage. He's the guy I'm working for. I also met his two kids, Erik (18) and Isabel (17). Worked late helping Ernst do carpentry, making desks for their Christian school.

Friday 18 January
Had a really good talk with a black guy called Simon McKenzie. He told me what he sees in South Africa.

Monday 21 January
Made three tables for the new primary school that starts tomorrow. Cut wood for the desks as well. Had to walk home because there was no ride.

Friday 25 January
There was a forest fire at Bizweni farm today. After work I went to the gym with Erik and a guy I'm working with called Cliffy. He's Coloured, but the gym said there was no colour coding. Went to youth in the evening. It consists of about 99 per cent Coloureds—we were the only whites bar one other.

Tuesday 29 January
Went to Crossroads township with Simon McKenzie and his wife in the afternoon, where I was able to ask questions of a group of people, with Simon interpreting. We then went to another part of Crossroads where Simon's mother lives. I interviewed two Christian guys there, one a pastor, and learned a lot from them. Drove past another very large shanty town called Khayalitsha on the way home.

Friday 1 February
Kobus said today he could use me here at Bizweni right up until I fly home—for the next six weeks. He wants me to organise getting more white people to come to youth.

Sunday 3 February
Played flute at church in the morning and went up to the front to tell the church what I'd been doing in South Africa.

Thursday 7 February
Worked at Bizweni until lunchtime, then Dave and Sandy Phillips took Sally and me right down the Cape Peninsula. It was incredible. We had a brilliant time.

Friday 8 February
A guy called Clive (a major in the army) picked me up from work and took me to Rusthof, a Coloured township, to stay with him and his wife, Karen, for a couple of weeks. They have two small boys, Roscoe and Kurt.

Sunday 10 February
Went for a walk along the Coloured beach in the afternoon. Went to a church meeting in the evening. I played a solo tonight in the worship.

Thursday 14 February

Tonight I went with Eugene to an ANC meeting. There were about 60 people there. During the meeting they had a question time so I raised my hand and told them about the different political ideas I'd seen all over the world. Then I told them how in the history of time no political system had ever been totally successful except a theocracy—like King David in the Bible succeeded in all he did when he obeyed God.

Friday 15 February

I spoke at youth tonight about what I saw in the youth group, what I saw in South Africa, what's going to happen here and how they can contribute to God's plan for the country. I'm totally flat broke as from today.

Tuesday 19 February

Today I designed and made two chairs for the preprimary school. Cliffy gave me R5 for petrol for my motorbike and on the way home I stopped to talk to Tommy, a guy from youth. He said he wanted to pay for my petrol for the rest of my stay here. Wacky, 'cos I'm broke!

Thursday 21 February

Carried on with making chairs today at Bizweni.

Saturday 23 February

Went to a street outreach with the youth in the morning, then helped set up the marquee at Bizweni for a wedding in the afternoon. I went to the wedding. The stage collapsed under the weight of the choir, and the groom burst into tears during the vows! Went with Greg and some others to the street racing on the freeway. They start at 1.30 am. I stayed until 3 am.

Monday 25 February

On Saturday God sent me money from some people in Durban, so I got the cheque cashed. Worked making chairs again. Then I had to stop because Kobus said a man was going to sue Bizweni for stealing his design. But I redesigned it so he would never be able to.

Saturday 2 March

Went with Winston and Charmaine to an all-day worship/praise conference. It wasn't very good. There was practically an argument at the end about whether someone can get saved by praise. Three out of the four speakers said, 'No.'

What a load of junk! I stood up and said that God inhabits the praises of his people. That means 'lives in'. God lives in my heart because praise comes from the heart. So when I praise I'm projecting God on to the people through my flute. God will save whoever he chooses, however he chooses.

In the evening we went to play crazy golf.

Friday 8 March
In the evening they had a supper party *(braai)* at Clive and Caron's for my leaving. All the youth came. They sang a song to me and all kinds of stuff. Some of it was pretty moving!

Tuesday 12 March
Went to Crossroads with Eugene and visited a crèche and a school. Took some pictures. Then went to Khayalitsha. Talked to lots of people there.

Thursday 14 March
Went to say goodbye to Kobus and Hazel. Then Sally, Erik, Eugene, Rhett and Cliffy took me to the airport. I arrived in Durban as 12.40 am. Peter van Niekerk met me and took me back to his place, where we had coffee and talked. I slept on the living room floor.

Tuesday 19 March
Peter, Natasha and Charene took me to the airport. The security was so tight because of the war in the Gulf that they weren't even allowed in the building. I boarded the plane at about 5.15 pm and flew first to Johannesburg and then home to England, arriving at 7.20 am on Wednesday 20 March 1991 in time for Dave and Sarah's wedding.

10

Help on its way

Simon groaned with the agony he felt in his leg. Why was it taking so long? When was something going to happen? It seemed like hours since the ambulancemen first arrived. What could they be up to?

One consolation: If they were spending so much time taking care of Vally, at least he must be alive, though he wasn't in the *bakkie*. He probably needed medical care a lot more than Simon.

Just when Simon was beginning to despair, the police arrived. They'd come from Eindekul, not far down the road, to direct traffic and take details of the accident.

At last, someone who could speak English—but only just.

'What's happening to the ambulancemen?' Simon asked one of them. 'My leg's hurting like crazy.'

'They will be here soon,' one of the policemen replied.

'Can you make sure my tapes aren't stolen when I'm in the ambulance?'

'Tapes?'

'Yes, my music tapes. They're really important to me, man. Do you think I could take them along?'

The policeman shook his head, not fully understanding the question, and moved off to direct traffic. Simon knew it was unlikely that he'd be able to take them, but they were important to him. At least it was worth a try.

Meanwhile Vally lay on the side of the road with serious neck injuries. The ambulancemen were working hard to stabilise his neck and shoulder ready for the ride to hospital.

Once Vally was safely in the ambulance, the men turned their attention to Simon, who by now was almost numb with the pain.

First they injected him with a painkiller and managed to put a splint on his broken leg. It hurt like crazy but as Simon always said about workout in the gym, 'No pain, no gain.'

Because of his huge size and the injuries he'd suffered, they had difficulty getting him out of the *bakkie*. Gradually, though, with a lot of heaving and shoving, they finally made it.

From his stretcher, Simon pointed to his music tapes, saying, 'Make sure my tapes don't get lost.'

Despite the language barrier they seemed to understand and passed him a few tapes from inside the *bakkie's* cab. They then loaded Simon into the ambulance and began the 20-minute ride to Piketberg Hospital.

By now the painkiller was taking effect. Simon's leg, though still painful, wasn't any longer the centre of all his attention.

When they arrived at Piketberg Hospital they were both unloaded from the ambulance and seen by a succession of doctors and nurses, who poked and prodded Simon. They gave him another painkiller, then talked among themselves about his condition and about what they could do.

Simon was lying there in the hospital for over an hour before being carried back to the ambulance. Once more they were off on a journey, this time apparently to the trauma unit at a hospital in Cape Town. For whatever reason, the medical staff at Piketberg Hospital had taken the decision that Simon's and Vally's injuries were serious enough to warrant the long, rough journey to Cape Town.

'Oh, well,' thought Simon. 'They must know what they're doing.'

Simon felt a stab of pain as the ambulance hit a bump in the road.

'Any chance of a drink of water?' he asked the nurse as nicely as he could. 'I'm gasping!'

'Water? No water!' the nurse replied. 'Wait until Cape Town.'

Simon sighed in defeat and relaxed once again, falling into that strange kind of half-awake, half-asleep state that many people experience on a journey.

Somewhere much further on the road to Cape Town, the sales rep José de Fratus was thinking about the accident he'd seen that day. The young driver who'd overtaken him seemed cheerful enough when José had spoken with him. How was he doing?

José's eyes filled with tears as he remembered his own son, aged 24, who'd died in a car accident near the de Fratus home nearly two years ago. A drunk driver had crashed into the car. He had died after being in a coma for 24 hours. As in Simon's case there wasn't a thing the young man could do.

For months after that, each time José travelled along that route in the course of his business he remembered Simon and wondered how he was doing.

Simon blinked several times and moved his head slightly to see the nurse sitting near him. The ambulance continued on its noisy journey, but everything inside the vehicle was strangely still and silent.

'How's Vally?' he whispered worriedly, gesturing to him on the other side of the ambulance.

'He is OK. Do not worry,' the nurse replied, struggling with the little English she had.

'Good,' Simon said. 'Only Vally's a great friend of mine and I don't want anything to happen to him.'

Friends. What would Simon do without them? Ever since he'd left school and started home study they'd become especially important.

11

Guinness scented socks

Simon first got to know Julien Haycock when Julien joined Simon's church in March 1987. They soon became good friends. But then for a year Julien was away from Bath, working in Wrexham with other Christian young people on a Go! Team.

Simon spent his days at home by himself supposedly doing his final studies for his GCSEs. Instead, he'd often phone Julien and the two of them would spend hours telling each other jokes. The Reynolds' phone bill soon reached astronomical proportions. But the jokes carried on unhindered.

When he'd finished his year in Wrexham, Julien returned to Bath, got a job and came to live with the Reynolds. He spent six months 'sharing a room with Simon's socks', as he described it. It was a small room and Julien copied Simon in sleeping on the floor.

The attic room they shared was ideal for keeping Guinness and lager at just the right temperature. They'd store their cache of canned Guinness between the slates and the plasterboards in the sloping ceiling, then drink them secretly in the dead of night.

Whenever he opened a can of Guinness late at night Simon would pour some of it on his smelly socks.

'What're you doing that for, Simon?' Julien asked once.

'Well, if my dad comes in and asks, "Can I smell beer?" I can say, "Yeah, it's me socks. Smell 'em."'

Simon and Julien used to get in trouble about once every week. One time in a church meeting Simon's dad was being prayed for at the front. The person praying for him had placed his hands on Peter's bald head.

'They're praying for hair!' said Julien in a very loud stage whisper. They both almost cracked up with laughing.

With Simon's concern for the vulnerable, the two of them decided to object to shops selling Tarot cards. They saw these as a subtle way of welcoming the influence of demons or evil spirits. They went into the first shop they knew sold the Tarot cards. Simon picked a pack off the shelf and plonked it down loudly on the counter.

'God doesn't like these,' he said bluntly.

They were ceremoniously thrown out.

At the next shop Julien decided that a more gentle approach would be better.

'These Tarot cards can really cause people problems,' he explained to the shopkeeper. 'As Christians we're worried that people are being confused and hurt by them.'

The result was a useful discussion on the merits and otherwise of Tarot cards.

For a few weeks after that, on a Sunday morning just before the teens meeting at their church, Simon and Julien would pray outside the local shop selling Satanist and witchcraft items. The result of all their prayer and activity was—the shop moved to bigger premises! Although they were discouraged, they didn't give up.

Often Simon and Julien would meet at lunchtimes and wander around the city centre eating Ben's Home-made Cookies. These were a great delicacy that came in loads of different flavours and cost the earth.

Julien and Simon worked together on a building site, doing a big contract for the supermarket chain Waitrose. Julien looked after Simon because, although he was big for his age, he was still very young. At lunchtime the men would go for a drink together. It was a very hot summer and Simon had a pint of beer and couldn't manage to walk straight, let alone work.

Simon and Julien went to an annual Christian holiday in Wales called the Bible Week. Simon called it Babe Week because there were so many girls there. For the week before Bible Week they did voluntary preparation work at what was known as pre-week. Simon and Julien called it Pub Week.

During Babe Week itself every girl Simon met was truly the one for him. Julien found it very funny that the girls

Simon fancied seemed to be shorter and shorter as the week progressed.

At the Bible Week Simon and Julien would go and sleep for a night on a big hill nearby, looking up at the stars. They'd take their sleeping bags and sleep in the open air, but the cold would wake them up again. Then they'd look up at the stars and Simon would raise a subject like UFOs and discuss it for half an hour before going back to sleep again.

At the Bible Weeks and during the rest of the year at times, Simon would often talk with Julien and other friends about the end times. He was intrigued by the stories of Frank Peretti—*The Prophet, This Present Darkness* and *Piercing the Darkness*.

Sometimes Simon and Julien would go to Bristol, buy a pizza and a big bag of popcorn and sit watching a movie in a big, air-conditioned cinema.

One time they were going to watch a film about the pop group U2 called *Rattle & Hum*. As usual, Simon had a big floppy jumper on, even though it was a very hot day. They wanted to have some lager with their pizza and popcorn so Simon tried smuggling in six cans stuck up his jumper.

It was no good. Simon was caught by the security guard. Instead of saying, 'I'm very sorry to try and sneak these in,' he decided to try it on. 'You couldn't keep them in the fridge for us, could you?' he asked politely. And the guard agreed!

When they finished watching the film they were handed six ice-cold cans of lager at the door.

Simon was taking himself much less seriously than before—thanks to his mum. His craziness rubbed off on to Julien.

'I was crazy before,' Julien told Simon once, 'but you've helped bring it out of me even more.'

Telling jokes was one of Julien's best ways of getting Simon to laugh. He told Simon one of his favourites:

'A missionary was walking through the jungle when he saw a lion approaching. Not knowing what else to do, the missionary got down on his knees to pray. After a few moments the missionary looked up to see the lion on its knees.

'"What are you doing?" asked the missionary.

'"I'm saying grace," came the reply.'

Julien knew that getting Simon to laugh meant that other people laughed, too. They watched *Bill and Ted's Excellent Adventure* and *Wayne's World* with some other friends. It was a scream with Simon's contagious laugh. Before they'd been out for more than a few minutes they wanted to go back in again. They saw those films again and again until they almost knew them by heart.

Simon and Julien were often in each others' pockets for money, though Julien claimed it was usually a case of Simon being in Julien's pockets 'cos Simon was broke.

They'd go to McDonalds together with Julien's money. Simon would have two Big Macs to Julien's one. After they'd finish they'd go up to the girl behind the McDonalds till and ask, 'Can I have a shake, please?' Then they'd both shudder from head to foot with her watching on with horror and amazement.

They used to stop and talk to buskers in Bath city centre. Simon would then start talking about Jesus. Sometimes he was a bit blunt and Julien would get really embarrassed, especially if he wasn't in the mood when Simon was. Simon was always in the mood to help the needy.

Before Simon left for South Africa Simon drove to Hereford to pick up Julien's nieces and bring them back to Bath to stay for a few days. On the way back there was a massive tailback coming up to the turn-off for Bath. Simon drove past everyone on the hard shoulder.

'Simon, there's police up there, directing the traffic,' Julien asked in horror. 'What're you going to do?'

'Leave it to me,' Simon replied.

He pulled up near the police and unwound the window.

'I've *got* to get these children to Bath,' he said with rising tension in his voice.

'Oh, right, sir,' the policeman said, stopping the traffic to let Simon through.

He managed to get away with it.

Simon recalled how he and Julien (or Jules as he often called him) had a special friendship. Despite the fact that Jules was older, they got on well together, Simon treating him as a big brother.

'Simon was my first friend ever,' Julien said once. 'I was a loner. Simon would say to me, "How are you feeling, Julien?" and I'd make a joke. Simon would sit on me and say, "I asked how are you feeling?" He kept on until I said how I was feeling. There must have been a 10-year age gap between us but I treat him like a big brother.'

They were very honest with each other. One time Julien made a cross out of wood and he was going to use it in a street mime to preach the gospel.

'Don't do it, Julien,' Simon said. 'It's naff.'

After getting over his disappointment, Julien abandoned the idea. 'If Simon says it's naff it really must be!' he said.

While Simon was in South Africa the first time he recalled getting a tape from Jules. He lay on his bed in Durban late one night listening to it through headphones and laughing his head off. It was a sound effects tape using lots of people from the church. Julien had held up a ghetto blaster with a tape in it and asked a girl in church, 'Don't you want to say something to Simon?'

'Hello, Simon, how are you?' she said, thinking it was a live link-up and expecting to hear Simon replying.

'No, Fiona, it's a tape.'

'Oh, right.'

Simon laughed and laughed when he heard all this on the tape they sent him. Then, when he returned to Bath, he and Jules were still buddies. But when they moved into a house together things started to go wrong. They ended up as 'sworn enemies', not having much to do with each other.

Eventually Simon returned for the second time to South Africa. Simon wrote to Julien:

That ever-growing friendship that just seemed to so naturally flow was, like, crushed to the size of a baby pea. What a mess! Even after I moved out of the house, things were never the same.

Simon remembered how he'd recorded some music over that original tape that had meant so much to him. While in South Africa this time he was playing it late one night when the music ended and the last five minutes of Jules' message was left.

Simon had nearly cried. It wasn't so much what Jules *said*. It was that it reminded him of how special Jules was to him. He'd thought of the whole sleepless, merciless nightmare in the Park Avenue house they'd shared together.

Peace only really moved in there when I left. Much as I'd like to shift the blame from my own conscience, I can't.

Jules, you've known me at my best and at my worst. And sometimes I can be the most arrogant, self-righteous little asshole that ever walked the face of the earth. I'm really sorry for being so stupid. My pride cost me a friendship that was one of the positive attributes to my life thus far.

I don't want to try and recreate or imitate what I've lost; I just want my friend back.

12

Fearsome foursome

The house in Park Avenue seemed such a good idea at the time. In 1991, after his return from South Africa, Simon shared the four-bedroom house with three others: Andy Theaker, Julien Haycock and Nathan Luckock. From time to time, over the 11 months they were together, other young people such as Nick Shepherd and Howie Kellett came to stay for short times.

'All of us were a bit odd in one way or another,' Andy recalled once. 'Simon was big and soft. He bent over backwards to help us, but there'd always be something to laugh at.'

Andy had a funny laugh and Simon spent much of his time trying to get him to burst out. That would set the others laughing. There usually wasn't anything particular to laugh about, but they all carried on anyway. Sometimes the four of them would spend the whole evening laughing their heads off.

One of the guys at the house expected everyone to be in bed by 10.00 pm. Simon would counter this by flicking on his stereo and starting to praise God at the top of his voice at 10.05. The guy would come and complain to Simon. Then Simon would get Andy to laugh, which would get everyone else laughing, and the problem would be deflated.

By choice, Simon went for the second smallest room in the house. He had a duvet on the floor—and that was it. His clothes were always in a heap spread over the rest of the floor. He'd take his dirty washing home to his parents occasionally to wash them there.

On his wall he had pinned up the skin of an African python, a treasured possession from Kenya. It was given to him by Ted Kent, a man of faith and a radical who went where others feared to go. Simon appreciated Ted's constant encouragement over the years and had grown up to follow in his footsteps. Ted had been a great help in making arrangements for Simon's first trip to South Africa.

Simon wore those Afghan slippers that were so popular 10 years ago. Even in summer he always had three or four layers of clothes on. Others in the house, even though they were single, described Simon as 'generally scruffy'.

The others found it amusing that Simon always slept on the floor, his feet poking out of the end of the duvet. He gave the impression that it was the natural thing to do. 'Doesn't everybody sleep on the floor?' he'd ask, knowing full well that it was unusual.

Andy and his fiancée, Sharon, found Simon easy to talk to. Although Simon was always laughing and joking, he knew when to be serious. They found Simon a good listener.

Nathan enjoyed Simon's irrepressible sense of humour. He laughed like a drain when Simon came to a fish party dressed as a hammerhead shark. Simon was decked out in black plastic bin liners and a Cossack hat with the flaps sticking out. It caused quite a sensation.

One time Simon, Nathan and some others went to Weston-super-Mare and just walked and walked around in the pouring rain singing at the tops of their voices. They were loud and crazy, running across the empty beach carefree and happy. Simon would shout, 'Steady Neddy!' very loudly and the whole group would burst into laughter.

Once they drove through Bath city centre in the dead of night with the music of Michael W Smith blaring out of the open car windows: *Hallelujah, for the Lord God Almighty reigns.'* Another time in Bristol Simon went to an ex-army shop and bought Nathan a greatcoat, something he treasured ever after that.

Simon, Nathan and some of the others would go up Solsbury Hill, mess around and have a bonfire, then toast marshmallows. They'd have a loud, happy time together. They'd take blankets to keep off the damp, then stay until late at night. Once when it was time to leave, Simon managed to hose down the bonfire singlehanded. Scots might have described it as a wee triumph!

Simon and Nathan both shared an enjoyment of music. Simon would play the flute and Nathan the violin. A favourite tune was *Amazing Grace,* with its beautiful, haunting melody.

One Sunday evening Simon and Nathan were walking to Simon Harrison's for a student meeting. All the way there they sang at the top of their voices:

Running over, running over,
My cup's full and running over.
Since the Lord saved me
I'm as happy as a bee.
My cup's full and running over.

It should have been 'I'm as happy as can be,' but they preferred their own lighthearted version.

Andy Theaker was several years older than Simon but treated him as a big brother. Simon relished this and offered Andy lots of advice.

Not only that, but Simon liked to help in practical ways whenever he could. Once Andy bought a huge bookcase from a demolished house. For ages he and a friend tried their best to get it into the house. Simon came along, saw what they were doing, then simply picked it up and carried it in singlehanded!

Simon's size and strength made furniture moving easy. That was one of the reasons why David Hansford, a family friend, asked him to drive through Europe to Genoa and help David to move his father plus his furniture back to England from his home in Sicily.

Simon ate like a horse. When they went to McDonalds the others would have a conventional meal while Simon would have two Big Macs and two large french fries. While the others politely had a couple of biscuits with their coffee, he'd sit and eat a whole packet of biscuits at one sitting. He'd have two or three bowls of cereal for breakfast. In terms of eating he could outdo anyone in the house.

Simon set an example to the others by being extremely friendly with everyone, including their neighbours on both sides. He'd also for ever be talking to down-and-outs in Bath, taking them out for a burger and telling them about God. His concern for the downtrodden and outcasts of society had been sharpened by his six-month visit to South Africa.

If the four guys went to a pub, Simon would be the noisiest one in the place. He'd be shouting, yelling and making a nuisance of himself. He gave the impression of being drunk, even though he might have only had one pint of beer.

When Simon first moved into the house he was an awful cook. He didn't have a clue. He was taking cooking lessons with his mum at home and he managed to learn how to make spaghetti bolognese. After that, Simon just lived on the stuff. Mince, mushrooms and tomatoes. He'd make it every night. He often burnt it and he never liked doing the washing up afterwards. He avoided such work like the plague.

At the advice of his church leaders before his planned return to South Africa, he spent the time seeking to get a qualification in civil engineering and building studies.

There was an unwritten rule that everyone in the shared house had to have a job in order to pay the rent. Simon wouldn't dream of going into a job centre. He just walked into Acer Engineering in Bath, asked for a job and was given one on the spot. They even sent him to college for a day and an evening a week. He hadn't been trained in design but he skilfully drew out various plans for collapsing quarries.

He loved that job. He was supposed to wear a shirt and a tie, but he managed to dress in his usual scruffy way. He'd mess up their photocopier, then try to fix it by taking it to pieces and get mucky into the bargain. He'd arrive home in the evening with black toner all over his shirt collar.

One lunchtime a week Simon went with his dad for a drink or a sandwich. Sometimes they'd go home and join with his mum, Barbie. He really enjoyed those times with his dad, whom he deeply respected. They would talk about a wide range of issues and Simon appreciated his dad's wisdom on matters. As Simon had grown through his teen years, their relationship had deepened until he saw his dad as an older friend in whom he could confide.

Simon was a film fanatic. His two favourite films at the time were *Terminator* and *Terminator 2,* starring Arnold Schwartzenegger as the robotic terminator. At work Simon would often use phrases from the film: *No problema, Trust me, Later, Hasta la vista, baby* (until we meet again), *Chill out, Eat me* and *I'll be back.*

Simon would suddenly spring into an office, even that of the director, with a rolled-up bundle of photocopies in his hand. He'd jump through the opening, roll over on the floor, go bang, bang, then say, '*Hasta la vista,* baby.'

He was for ever ringing up his Egyptian friend Hanney, making up tragic stories as if someone had died, or speaking in mock Egyptian. He enjoyed the reaction he got from onlookers.

One young lady in Acer Engineering was at the same level as Simon. He was getting paid more than she was and he complained to the boss about that being unfair. He persisted and they respected him for it. As a result, they put her salary up to his level, though he would have been willing to take a cut to be level with hers.

At least one of his colleagues at Acer realised that his brand of Christianity had a 'big smiling face on it'.

At the time of his being in the house Simon was into a mixture of worship music and heavy rock. There was an Australian group he particularly liked called *Midnight Oil.* He spent a lot of his free time reading the Bible and writing poetry.

Simon's main ambition during the time at the house was to return to South Africa. Everything in his room—the map on the wall, the clothes he wore, much of the music he liked—was to do with South Africa. He was strongly antiracist.

His hatred of racism extended to his home city of Bath. It didn't matter what age, sex or ethnic origin a person was, nothing bugged him about other people. He was comfortable with people of all backgrounds, old people as well as children.

Living together in the Park Avenue house combined some of the best and worst of times. When the guys first moved in together, Simon felt strongly that all four of them should sit down and eat together. One of the others joked that his reason for this was that he couldn't cook!

The trouble was, their lives were so very different that they couldn't find a slot in their day to sit down together. Simon would get annoyed that the others weren't expressing a common life together. The others couldn't see it like that. This led to a lot of friction later on.

In Simon's family he had always known regular 'family councils' where each member of the family could have his or her say. Family council was also the place for resolving issues. This meant that hurts and disappointments in others weren't left to fester. At the shared house, things weren't the same, and Simon found that frustrating.

Simon could be stubborn at times. Money was a source of contention. He was paid monthly and would generally run out of money within two and a half weeks.

He found it difficult to handle being paid monthly. Because he was so generous, he'd buy people burgers and drinks. He'd bring tramps home and get them something to eat from the fridge. He'd spend his money on chips and a dip rather than pooling the money. Then he'd wonder where his money had disappeared to.

When it came to rent time he'd have run out of money.

'Oh, I bought some new tapes. Cool,' he'd say with a smile.

This got the others really annoyed. They'd have to chip in money to bail him out until his next pay day. Then the whole saga would start again. Like the others, Simon was learning to relate to other people in life, especially in areas such as handling money.

In the end the four of them had a meeting to thrash out some of their grievances. Subjects ranged from money, food and washing-up to spending time together and praying with each other.

Eventually, the fearsome foursome went their separate ways and found other places to live.

13

Smelly Egypt

Simon's mind drifted back to the time he first met Hanney Ishak, an Egyptian student, in the college dining room in Bath. Hanney had only just arrived in the city and was looking a bit bewildered.

Lunch over, Simon hung around waiting for a chance to speak to him. The trouble was, it was difficult, even for Simon, to know what to say to a complete stranger.

Finally, plucking up his courage, Simon went over to where Hanney was sitting.

'Hi. I'm Simon.'

'Hello. My name's Hanney.'

Pause.

'So—er—you're Egyptian, are you?'

'Yes. I lived in Egypt until recently.'

Pause.

Suddenly, Simon remembered he'd heard something recently about Egypt. *Now, what was it?*

'I understand Egypt smells,' he said suddenly.

'Is that right?'

'That's what I've heard.'

'Well, it's true. There *are* places in Egypt that smell. But it's disgusting thinking about Egypt as a smelly place.'

Like a fish rising to the bait, Simon rose to Hanney's remark.

'No, I think it's disgusting you've come here from such a smelly place,' Simon said casually.

As soon as he'd opened his mouth he regretted the words, but it was too late. Making some feeble excuse, Simon beat a hasty exit before he could do any more damage.

After that, he couldn't sleep for nearly a week. Inside, he was kicking himself for saying such a flippant, crazy thing. OK, he only meant it for a bit of fun, but such racist remarks weren't likely to make him any friends. Instead of *How to Win Friends and Influence People,* it was more a case of *How to Lose Friends and Insult People.*

Sunday came round and who should be in church but Hanney! Simon agonised over the decision to say sorry to Hanney. It wasn't something that came naturally. Even as a child he'd always had problems asking forgiveness of other people.

Finally, plucking up courage yet again, he went up to his would-be friend who by now was probably his enemy.

'Look, Hanney, about last week . . .'

'Last week?'

'Yeah, you know, what I said about you coming to this country.'

'Oh, *that,'* Hanney said with a laugh. 'Don't worry about that.'

'Look, I'm really sorry. I didn't mean . . .'

'Forget it, Simon. I'm just glad we got to know each other.'

'Thanks for understanding, Hanney. You know, I haven't slept all week because of it.'

'Oh, Simon, what a waste of energy!'

By now they were both laughing. A sort of bond of friendship had begun to grow between them, despite what Simon saw as a very poor start.

That Sunday Simon's mum, Barbie, was the preacher. Despite her age (she must have been at least 40 at the time), Simon reckoned she was pretty neat as a mum. She looked young and had auburn hair. Sometimes she could easily pass as Simon's sister.

'See the lady in the front with the white cardigan?' Simon asked, pointing to his mother.

'I think so,' said Hanney.

'That's my mum.'

Hanney glanced along the front row until he spotted this tall, well built lady.

'Oh, I think I see her. *That's* your mum?'

'Right. Cool, isn't she?'

'Yes.'

At the end of the church service, Simon couldn't help himself.

'Look, Hanney, you've *got* to come to my house for dinner.'

'Oh, no, Simon. I couldn't put you to any trouble.'

'No trouble at all. There's always loads to eat.'

'But what about your parents?'

'They won't mind a bit.'

'Not even having a smelly Egyptian?' Hanney said with a laugh.

'Not even having a smelly Egyptian!'

Back at the house, when Hanney was introduced to Simon's parents, he just couldn't believe it.

'This is *your* mother?' Hanney asked incredulously.

'Yeah. Remember? I pointed her out to you.'

'Oh, no. The lady I thought you pointed out was much more like you, Simon. She was much larger and perhaps—er—older looking than your mother.'

'Who else had a white cardigan on today?' Barbie asked.

'Margaret! So you thought my mum was Margaret?'

The household collapsed into laughter. Simon was nearly in tears with amusement that Hanney thought Margaret was his mum. Hanney could see the funny side of it and joined in the side-splitting laughter.

After that, Simon sort of took Hanney under his wing. He introduced him to people all over Bath, made him feel at home and helped him loosen up a bit.

Even though he was only three years older than Simon, Hanney was one of those guys who were labelled 'sensible' and 'mature'. By contrast, Simon liked to be free and spontaneous. The two quickly hit it off and within a few months Simon and Hanney decided to join forces and rent an apartment together. It was a pleasant two-bedroom place near the city centre.

Hanney knew about the previous disaster Simon had been through in sharing a pad with others, but it didn't seem to bother him. Simon was glad about that. He really wanted to learn how to fend for himself, especially with his return to South Africa looming ever closer.

For ten months the two of them shared the apartment. They had their off days and their arguments, but Simon was learning to give as well as take.

They were completely different in most respects. Simon was very big. Hanney was very small. Hanney was quiet. Simon was loud. Simon would go out and hire several videos and a huge takeaway. Hanney would ask, 'What are you doing? How much did all this cost you?' Hanney was sensible. Simon was crazy.

As always, Simon loved to entertain people. He'd invite the local homeless people in for a meal, at times much to Hanney's surprise. One was a black guy called Fred, who came from Ghana.

Simon wasn't the world's greatest cook. At the previous house he'd learned to do spaghetti bolognese. Here with Hanney, his speciality was baked potatoes with chilli con carne. He'd make mountains of it, then invite everyone he could to come and polish it off.

'Me and Hanney just love food, don't we, Hanney?' he'd say.

Hanney was one of the few people to see how sensitive and easily hurt Simon was, despite his bravado. The two of them would have their arguments. One or the other would do or say something that would offend. But Simon remembered how easy it was to say sorry to Hanney. He was such a forgiving sort of person. For himself, Simon never held any grudges. He liked to forgive and forget.

Simon always liked a nice long (in both senses of the word) lie in the bath. That was fine when he lived at home and there were two toilets. But when he and Hanney shared an apartment, there were inevitable clashes.

There was the time when Hanney came home while Simon was in the bath and pounded on the door.

'What d'ya want?'

'Hurry up, Simon. I need the toilet.'

'Can't you wait? I'll only be another few minutes.'

'No, I can't. I'm desperate.'

'Well, can't you do it in a bottle, then?'

'No. Where am I supposed to find a bottle?'

'Oh, I don't know. Try under your bed. It's where the psychiatrist kept his wife 'cos he thought she was a little potty.'

Silence.

'Hanney? Are you there?'

Silence.

'Hanney? *Hanney!*'

Oh, no, he must have misheard the word 'bed' and peed all over it or something!

Panic propelled Simon out of his bath and into some of his clothes. Still half dressed, he fumbled with the door lock and rushed out.

'You all right, Hanney?'

'Sure.'

'You didn't pee all over the bed, did you?'

'What do you take me for, Simon? Of course I didn't.'

At last, Simon breathed a sigh of relief and returned to get the rest of his clothes on. But that night before he settled down to sleep on the floor he felt Hanney's duvet to make sure it wasn't wet.

Simon remembered another funny incident with Hanney. It was a hot day and Simon was on his way out. He rushed into the bathroom and turned on both taps. Then he scooped up a double handful of water and splashed it all over his face. Instead of the usual refreshing sensation, the water felt thick and his eyes began to sting.

A glance in the mirror and he shouted out with shock. His whole face was covered in black hairs. Hanney came running to see what the fuss was all about. He almost died laughing.

'Sorry, Simon,' Hanney said as he took a breath, 'I had a haircut and washed my hair in the basin. I must have forgotten to rinse it out!'

The lease on the apartment came to an end and the rent was put up. That meant that both Simon and Hanney had to move out. Simon had enjoyed his time living in the same place as Hanney and was looking forward to moving in as a lodger with a fun couple from the church.

14

Laughing landlady

Simon's new landlady, Diana Musters, was great fun. Simon lived at Rod and Diana's house for the few months before going to South Africa for the second time.

His packed lunches were enormous. Diana used to make him four big rolls, cake, yoghurt, fruit, drink and two or three chocolate biscuits.

Each day his work colleagues would open his lunchbox and if they didn't know what was in one of his bread rolls they'd take a bite. If they didn't like it they'd put the roll back in and stick the lid on. If they liked it they'd pay him for it!

Diana reckoned he was too fussy about expiry dates. One time she gave him a yoghurt that was one day past its expiry date. He put a cross on it to indicate that it couldn't be eaten and left it untouched in his otherwise empty lunchbox.

Diana loved playing tricks on Simon. The day after the rejected yoghurt incident she put talcum powder on his sausage roll to make it look mouldy. She also made him an egg sandwich and wrote on it, 'Apologies. This egg smells like drains. I hope it tastes all right.' When his workmates opened his lunchbox to check it, instead of taking a bite out of each roll, they left a little note saying, 'Good luck, Simon. *Bon appetite.*'

He brought his lunchbox home empty.

For breakfast on a Saturday he'd have a mountainous pizza and a huge bowl of cereal. He also had an enormous main meal each evening.

One morning he wanted Weetabix and the box was empty. The next day Diana put a substitute in the empty box. Suddenly there was an enormous shout from downstairs as, bleary eyed, Simon discovered the truth.

His bedroom was as usual an absolute tip. The carpet couldn't be seen. Diana always commented on his noticeboard, which was full of pictures of people going through hard times, hungry African children, poor peasants in South America, pictures that tugged at her heartstrings. He slept under a mountain of ten blankets and rugs with the window wide open, even on the coldest night.

He would warn everyone when he was about to have a bath. That meant the bathroom was out of use for two hours. Diana could always tell Simon's mood by the tapes he played. If he played melancholy tapes, it would take a long time for her to clean the windows. He'd play a tape with mournful music on the pan pipes and tears would flow down her face. Then when he played cheery, fast songs her windows would be cleaned in extra quick time.

He enjoyed reading his poetry to Diana and her husband Rod. He expressed his deep compassion for other people in poetry. He'd write down a line or a phrase as it came to him, keeping it on file. Then eventually, from the components, he'd compile the final poem or song.

He was perceptive for his age. As a 17-year-old he'd written a tribute to an unborn baby.

I put this poem together shortly after I learned how a baby, while still in her mother's womb, can distinguish the difference between the voices of her father and mother,' he explained. 'An unborn baby can also sense tension, experience fear and hence become anxious even before birth. How much more care then should we take in protecting a child's mind before she leaves the security and comfort of her first home!

I'm lying here awake again.
There's a ringing in my ears.
It's the sound of Mummy's crying.
I can picture her tears.

Daddy's shouting words at her
That I don't understand.
I feel him getting closer now,
And the back of his hand.

Every day and every night
I feel my mummy's pain.
Mummy's love is silent,
And Daddy's is in vain.

My home is built of tension
In the absence of any trust.
I'm too afraid to leave here,
But I know one day I must.

Will I become a companion
To heartbreak and fate?
Do I still have a hope,
Or is it too late?

Will I be safe with Daddy,
Or from him will I run?
Will Mummy persevere,
Or get me over and done?

The lonely child walks into the world.
Behind her broken smile there's a pain untold.
The love that was shown to the heart that was broken,
The things unknown were the things unspoken.

During his time at his landlady's house Simon had his usual favourite clothes, including one jumper with holes in that he almost lived in. He'd put his thumbs through enormous holes at the bottom of the sleeves. They were like gloves. He'd go to church like that, all tatty, and Diana would suggest he tidy himself up a bit.

In the end Diana thought his jumper was too terrible for words. She chopped off the string sleeves, mended them and washed the jumper, all without telling Simon.

'Simon,' she announced one evening, 'your jumper's shrunk.'

When he saw it his face fell. 'What *have* you done to it?' he cried in despair. 'My *favourite* jumper. You can't do this to me.'

That year Diana used Simon's huge socks as Christmas stockings. But some of them were too far gone. She said to him once, 'Simon, you're going to be missing some of your socks.' They were all full of holes. She would take away some of the old socks and replace them secretly with unmarked ones left behind at the school she worked for.

'Oh, no, I don't need them,' he'd say but didn't really mean.

His landlady wondered how he ever managed to find his way into his boxer shorts, they had so many holes in! It was almost better to wear nothing than some of his boxer shorts. He always insisted they were fine. He had one shirt with no buttons on at all.

'What's the good of this?' Diana asked him.

'It's my favourite,' he replied defensively.

The truth was, *he'd* expanded but his shirt hadn't. One day she was ironing it—it had probably never been ironed before—and she sewed on a whole new set of buttons.

He let out a yell from upstairs, 'You've ruined my shirt!'

She replied, 'You don't even wear it.'

He had so few shirts he had to wear them all.

He had a Russian Cossack hat and greatcoat that made him look quite threatening. Diana took the coat off him, mended the lining and sent it to the cleaners. After that he complained, 'It smells clean. It's just not the same anymore.'

He got on well with Diana's husband, Rod, a physicist, who liked to do research into everything. Simon and Rod would chew over something for hours, discussing their views on a particular subject. He acted as a stimulus to Rod.

Simon hardly had any possessions. They weren't important to him. For him, money spent on clothes was a waste. Far better to invest it in buying something for homeless people. When he'd been 16 he'd gone on holiday to Florida with a family he knew. Even the materialism he saw there didn't attract him. But if anyone touched his tapes they'd be in real trouble.

Sometimes he'd go out in the dead of night to spend time with the down-and-outs in the streets of Bath. Occasionally he even shared a bedspace with them and would return to his landlady's in the morning stinking.

Sometimes he took his flute and joined in with the buskers, not to make money but to identify with them. He'd bring them back and some of them would stink to high heaven. She went round afterwards wiping everything they touched.

He loved inviting friends round for a meal or for the evening. One time he suddenly asked Diana if she could put up eight people because they'd just come over from South Africa. They all ended up sleeping on the floor.

Simon became renowned for his sleep-overs. He'd get a couple of videos—Simon and Rod had the same liking for videos—and then he'd spread the word that there was a sleep-over. All Simon's friends would bring food and drink, watch a couple of videos, then spend the night sleeping on the floor, the girls in one room, the boys in another.

Some young people next door to Diana's were always in trouble with the police, stealing cars and generally causing a nuisance. Simon had a bike that he'd scrimped and saved to buy. It was really special to him because it was his means of getting to work. He left it in the porch for five minutes and it was gone.

Simon was furious. He thrust his Cossack hat on to his head, even though it was summer, and stormed next door. The guy next door knew who'd taken it. As a result, Simon got his bike back. The only damage was that a mudguard was missing.

Feeling kind towards him, Diana cut up a plastic lemonade bottle and made a temporary mudguard for him. He used to ride almost to work, then take it off and put it in his rucksack in case his friends saw it and laughed. For those last couple of hundred metres it sometimes meant he had to put up with mud splattering all up his back.

The only problem living with Diana and Rod was the dog next door. The family there had a ferocious Alsatian that made their other dog, a Rottweiller, seem tame by comparison! Simon kept his bike in the garden shed until this Alsatian suddenly realised that Simon was scared of dogs. As soon as Simon approached, he literally tore part of the fence down so he could get through and chase Simon. This happened two or three times before Simon decided never again to keep his bike in the back.

Diana tried to encourage him to get over his fear by stroking the dog.

'I'd rather keep my hand, thanks very much,' he'd say.

Although he was scared of dogs, he loved Jyoti, a golden Labrador belonging to the Reynolds family. When he was at home he often took her for very long walks.

Once he managed to thumb a ride—on a bike! That was some achievement, as Diana later told her friends.

When Simon answered the phone Diana would dread what would happen this time. Once, a lady was phoning Diana because she'd been given her number by their son in Manchester. The two men in the respective families both had Parkinson's disease. She wanted to ask some advice and help but was a bit apprehensive about phoning.

Simon answered the phone with a perfect Chinese accent! He spoke on and on, talking absolute rubbish with this beautiful singsong accent.

The lady at the other end asked, 'Is this the Musters household.'

'Ah, so, it is indeed.'

'Do they—er—have any connections with Manchester?'

'Ah, so.'

Diana finally snatched the phone off Simon and tried to make amends. The lady at the other end quizzed her for ages. Who was that Chinese person? How was her husband? Was he ill in any way? It took about 10 minutes for Diana to convince her she had the right number. Simon loved it.

Another time he picked up the phone and said very loudly, '*What now?!*'

Simon embarrassed Diana many times. They'd be driving into the city centre to go to the church meeting and he'd suddenly stick his head out of the car window and yell out to a crowd of people in his booming voice: 'Jesus loves you!' Diana just hoped they didn't take down the registration number of the car!

Simon adored girls yet he got confused. 'Just friends,' was one of his favourite sayings, yet it was obvious to everyone else that he was absolutely infatuated with the girl.

He'd said goodbye to one girl at 2.30 in the morning and was walking back—the longest way, up a very steep hill for a couple of miles. Above him a helicopter directed its searchlight on to Simon. It followed him all the way up the hill and home, just on the outskirts of Bath. It hovered as he opened the gate and kept its searchlight on him as he went through the front door.

Simon came out again, looked up and yelled out loudly, 'Thanks. Bye!'

'Wow, you'd never believe it,' Simon told Diana, who was still up, waiting for him. 'Even Royalty don't get this treatment.'

Apparently there'd been an incident at the university and the police saw this tall guy walking on his own in the dead of night and wanted to check what he was up to.

'It was a privilege having Simon to stay,' said Diana after Simon had returned to South Africa. 'I don't think I've ever laughed so hard in all my life.'

15

Saxophone busker

Simon used to love wandering the streets of his home city of Bath. Bath is situated on the River Avon in a natural amphitheatre of steep hills. The city is built of local limestone and is one of the most elegant and distinguished of British cities. It gets its distinction from the wealth of classical Georgian buildings mounting the steep valley sides.

The hot mineral springs on the site attracted the Romans in AD 43, who over the space of 30 or 40 years drained the marsh, contained the steaming water in a reservoir and founded Bath as Aquae Sulis, dedicated to the deity Sulis Minerva, the goddess of healing.

The Saxons built the abbey on the site at which Edgar, first king of England, was crowned. The Normans rebuilt the church between 1088 and 1112.

Bath shared in the west of England wool trade and later in the cloth trade. But the baths, though still used by royalty, were poorly maintained.

In its heyday as a fashionable resort, the Elizabethan city of Bath was rebuilt and extended in Palladian style by the architects John Wood and Ralph Allen.

As the leading centre of English high society outside London in the 18th and early 19th centuries, Bath is rich in literary associations. Jane Austen's novels *Northanger Abbey* and *Persuasion* (both 1817/18) portray with delicate satire the keen perception of fashionable life in Bath around 1800.

Close to the abbey is the 18th century pump room, giving access to the hot springs and the Roman baths. Where 300 years ago Daniel Defoe described the area as a centre for raffling, gambling and levity, there are buskers plying their trade in the Abbey Churchyard, overshadowed by the 17th century abbey.

Here Simon loved to stop and spend time with the buskers. Sometimes he brought his flute and joined with them. At other times he would take them for a meal or introduce them to his friends from the church.

One busker Simon got to know especially well was Jorge Winiss Mabuza, a 31-year-old saxophone player from Mozambique. His music, Tuffo, was a traditional dance music from north Mozambique. Jorge played saxophone and percussion.

In July 1991 Jorge and his band Eyuphore had travelled from Maputo, Mozambique, to Johannesburg, South Africa. From there they went via Frankfurt, Germany, to Sweden and Norway, doing various gigs before arriving in Britain.

When his band went back to Africa, Jorge stayed behind, for a time as an illegal immigrant. He then went to the Home Office, declared his position and sought political asylum. He had once been a political prisoner in his home country and he knew the dangers of returning home. He settled down in Bristol and started exploring the towns and cities around there.

One day Jorge visited Bath city centre and was amazed to hear the quality of music of the buskers there. One busker he met was Hum, a guitarist from Cardiff. They decided to team up and together regularly went busking in the abbey courtyard. Jorge enjoyed making a beautiful sound, even if he didn't make very much money.

One day Simon and his friend James came along. Simon listened for a while.

'Hey, that's a cool sound,' Simon said. 'Where are you from?'

'From Mozambique near South Africa.'

'I'm from South Africa,' he replied. It wasn't strictly true, but at least he'd lived there for six months.

Jorge misunderstood him. 'So, you're South African?'

'No, not really. I'm from Bath. But I lived there a while back.'

'I see.'

'And I feel African, you know, man?'

They started talking about Africa, music and other things of mutual interest. Simon listened as Jorge told him about how he got to the UK and about his group.

A few days later Simon and his two sisters came to see Jorge while he was busking. Simon talked about the church he went to. He invited Jorge to church and to coffee afterwards.

'It made me feel special that he should invite me,' Jorge recalled later. He had been in a church back in Mozambique. He had converted from Catholicism in 1986 when he found his own faith in Christ while he was a political prisoner for 17 months.

'We weren't allowed to have paper or a pen in prison, but I was somehow allowed to take in a Bible,' he said. 'I read it and decided to receive Christ.'

Simon took Jorge to the church meeting. Jorge had such a cool time that he never did get around to having a cup of coffee.

He told Simon about a dream he'd had.

'In my dream I saw a big church full of friendly people here in Bath. This seems to be the church I was dreaming about.'

'Wow, Jorge,' Simon replied, 'that's cool.'

Later, Jorge developed shingles and Simon and James decided to pray for him. While they were praying Simon asked God to use Jorge's saxophone playing to an even greater extent.

Normally, shingles lasts a long time but Jorge was free from all pain within two weeks.

'I'm completely better, Simon!' Jorge said excitedly.

'Yeah, that's God all right,' Simon replied, sharing his enthusiasm.

Simon helped Jorge in other ways, too. The Home Office authorities were giving him a hard time as a political asylum seeker. They said that if he didn't get a proper job he couldn't stay in Britain. Simon supported him through the difficult time.

Simon talked with Jorge about baptism, showing him that it was important for Christians to be baptised to enjoy God's full blessing. Later, when Simon had gone to South Africa, Jorge was baptised and wrote to tell Simon about it. Simon was planning to visit Jorge's friends in Africa. They had sent Jorge a Bible in the Changana language.

One day Simon watched Jorge playing outside the pizza house, then said, 'Come in and have a pizza. You'll enjoy it.'

Over the meal Simon told Jorge about his return to South Africa and invited him to a special farewell party. Jorge never showed up.

The next day he apologised to Simon, saying he felt sorry he hadn't come.

'That's OK,' Simon replied. 'But they're praying for me at church before I leave. You must come.'

'OK, I'll be there,' Jorge said.

Jorge said after Simon left for South Africa:

Travelling from Africa to Europe led to a gap between me and God. Simon helped me to bridge that gap.

At first Simon doubted if I was a genuine Christian. I was in the desert spiritually before I met him. Then he invited me to church and I felt so important. He kept telling me to catch the bus on a Sunday morning from Bristol to Bath. People thought I was crazy. 'How are you going to do that, man?' But I decided to do it because of Simon and because of his link with God.

I loved his sense of humour. When I heard him play the flute I said, 'Wow! That's good.' He loved the fact that he'd kept secret from me the fact that he was a musician, too. He was delighted that I enjoyed his little surprise.

16

Long road home

Once more Simon slowly came back to the harsh reality of a noisy ambulance on a bumpy road somewhere near Cape Town. Looking up he could see the South African nurse caring for Vally.

'How is he?' he asked.

'It is OK. It is OK,' the nurse replied soothingly in her broken English, not really understanding what he was saying. 'This is Cape Town.'

By now his tongue was sticking to the roof of his mouth. It seemed as if he'd been in a desert for weeks without water. Was it worth asking the nurse yet again?

'Water,' he said weakly. 'Water.'

'No water,' the nurse replied firmly.

Simon groaned with frustration as a sharp pain shot through his chest. He'd got used to the pain of his leg and arm, but this pain was somehow different and a bit frightening. What could it mean? Still, the doctors would be taking a look soon.

The nurse leaned over Simon and checked his pulse, using the watch she had pinned to the front of her outfit. She smiled down at Simon and he gave a faint flicker of recognition back.

He was going back to sleep again. He wanted to stay awake, but somehow it was out of his control. He wanted a drink, too. And he wished this whole nightmare journey was over so he could get back to Deon's place.

It was good to have friends in South Africa. Simon's best friend, though, was someone who at one time he didn't get on with at all.

17

Party on!

Simon was 10 when James Porter and his family moved to Bath. Even though they were in the same church youth group together, they hated each other. Everything Simon did annoyed James. Simon would deliberately rub James up the wrong way.

It was only in 1989 that Simon and James became close friends. Simon's friend Steve Musters worked with James at Portico Designs in Bristol. When Steve went to Tanzania for three months Simon went to do some temporary work in Portico Designs packing boxes of greeting cards.

That evening after work Simon and James were given a lift to Bath and were dropped off in the city centre.

'Why don't you come round to my parents' house for a meal?' James asked.

'Right, OK,' Simon replied.

In typical Simon style they decided to walk the three miles or so to James's house and on the journey they became the best of friends. They talked about absolutely everything they could think of—the lack of spiritual enthusiasm in the church, all the things they thought should be happening but weren't and the things that were happening that shouldn't. They disagreed strongly on a number of the issues, and that appealed to Simon.

From then on they spent almost every spare minute together. There wasn't a subject they couldn't discuss together, even if one of them knew the other would disagree.

For instance, there was the subject of sexual desires. Simon found masturbation a difficult subject to discuss. James asked Simon if he battled with it and whether he thought it was right or wrong. They both went red because they'd never talked about it before.

Simon finally admitted, 'Yes, I battle with it like most other guys. But I don't have all the answers at the moment.'

They talked about end times, deliverance and demons. Discussion about swearing came later on after he'd returned from South Africa the first time.

Simon and James were always broke. James wasn't earning very much, and all Simon's money was going into paying the rent on the house he shared with three others. Their main pastime was wandering around the centre of Bath in the dead of night making silly noises at people.

Simon would suddenly go up to someone and say, 'Hi! How're you doing?' They'd look bemused because they didn't know who he was. James would get really embarrassed. He did his best to get his own back by embarrassing Simon, but nothing was too whacky for Simon.

One evening James parked his parents' car in the main street and they wandered around for a bit, just being silly. When they came back to the car they decided to make out as if they were breaking into it. James unlocked the car and they both started jiggling the handles up and down.

Just then, around the corner came a whole group of people. They saw what Simon and James were doing and thought they were a couple of drunks. They tackled them, started swearing at them and told them they shouldn't be drinking and driving.

Simon and James were so shocked by this confrontation that they had to sit in the car for a while just to get their adrenaline back under control.

As on other occasions, they hadn't touched a drop of alcohol.

They went to the pub quite a bit. James hated the kind of pubs Simon liked—the ones with bikers, druggies and alcoholics. James would normally have been scared in those kind of places but Simon enjoyed being his big 'guardian angel'.

But their fun didn't depend on drink. It was fun simply walking around town making out they were drunk.

James, who helped lead a teens group at church, suggested once that Simon would be good with teenagers.

'No way!' he said. 'I wouldn't know what to do.'

Simon's lack of courage as a child had now gone full circle. He wasn't scared of anybody. He and James would be walking along at 11.00 at night and there'd be a dozen or so teenagers sitting in a park. He'd go up to them, say, 'Hi!' and he and James would sit down and talk with them.

Often they didn't have the courage to say anything about God, but sometimes they got so hyped up they could tell people about anything. They'd then often have a really good conversation about Christianity.

Early one evening Simon, James and Colin Medus were walking in the Colonnades when they came across 15 or so teenagers sitting around doing nothing. As they approached, they agreed together to invite them to church.

Simon went up to them and said, 'Hi, how are you? What're you doing tomorrow?'

'Dunno. Why?'

'D'ya want to come to church?'

The others were cringing at Simon's blunt approach but it worked, at least that time. They had an exceptionally good conversation with the kids that lasted for a couple of hours. The result was that two of the girls came to church the following day. By then their excitement and brashness had worn off, so they introduced them to two other girls in the church teens group and left them to it.

For Simon the blunt approach was the best way. What was the point in beating about the bush? After all, Jesus never made friends with people first!

Simon's bluntness rubbed off on to James. One time he was driving to Simon's place. He had to stop at traffic lights, saw two girls and instinctively said hello to them out of the window of the car. It was the only time in his life he'd ever done something like that. They looked astonished at first but then asked for a ride.

They got into the car and James said, 'Where would you like to go?'

'We'll just go where *you* want to go.'

'Well, I was off to meet my friend, Simon. We're going out somewhere.'

When they arrived at the apartment James decided to get his own back on Simon. He got the two girls to knock on the door while he hid behind a pillar. Simon came to the door. One of the girls, an extremely good looking one called Hayley, pretended she knew Simon.

Simon was absolutely gobsmacked, not knowing what to do. Eventually it dawned on him that James was playing a practical joke. James appeared from behind the pillar, laughing for all he was worth.

After spending time together, James dropped off the two girls in the centre.

A couple of weeks later Simon and James were walking in a recreation park at about 2.00 in the morning. Suddenly they came across two guys bent over a girl lying on the ground. The guys were looking panicky because the girl had had absolutely loads to drink. She was vomiting everywhere and seemed emotionally disturbed. It turned out to be the same girl, Hayley, James had picked up in the car.

Simon's immediate reaction was to start praying for her. One of the guys was very supportive of the idea of praying for her. In the end Simon and James managed to take Hayley home.

Simon and James were friendly with many of the buskers and new age travellers who visited Bath. They'd stop to talk with them, give them what money they could and help them in other ways. Simon's concern for the outcasts of society had influenced James as well.

For 18 months Simon and James were separated by thousands of miles while James studied a degree in drums at a university in the USA. On Sunday 27 October 1991 Simon recorded a tape to send to James:

OK, let's rock and roll, dude. Man, I can't wait for you to come back. I've just got so much to tell you. James, you're my closest buddy. There's no one going to take your place. There's no one closer. It's like—I can't even describe it—it's like God's given the two of us a friendship that's so special.

I miss you, pal. I just can't wait till you come back. I don't have anybody I can say to, 'How's it going?' Hurry back, pal. Come back and let's get on with some stuff. Worship and praising—I absolutely love it.

There's some things I need to get rid of, like being argumentative. I do it to start off with as a joke in a group setting. I pick on something somebody says. Someone goes, 'What do you think, Simon?' As I argue

*and feel the aggression come back at me, my
argument gets more and more beefy. I really get into it.
Not with a bad attitude. But I get to thinking, 'Is that
really good?'*

*Like I really shot out of the sky this Egyptian at one
of the student lunches at Simon Harrison's. He didn't do
or say anything wrong. I just shot him down. I was just
joking, messing around. I went back to him later and
said, 'Look, I'm really sorry.' He was so funny. He's such
a cute little guy. He said, 'Thank you for coming back
to me. I didn't take it wrong. You were a little bit over
the top but I didn't take any offence by it. The fact that
you came back to me really says something about you
and about this church.' I went, 'Yeeeeah! Rock and roll.
I'll do that again. I'll go and apologise. It's really good.'*

*There's so much God's showing me. What I want to
be is just so close to him. I want to be constantly
thinking and spouting out things from the Bible. I want
to be living it so every word I speak is based on a
biblical truth.*

*Going into South Africa fresh I could see that the
violence was wrong. There's something we can do. It's
not the way it should be. I—ah, man—I just love those
people. I just want to be there. I want to get into those
townships and to actually work on that farm with them
and become one of them. They couldn't understand for
ages, but once they understood I was with them, I had
a laugh with them. So I want to go back out there and
live.*

*I want to get married and have a family before Jesus
comes back, which I reckon will be soon. I guess it's all
in God's timing and he'll sort it out.*

*From all the prophecies I've had, it says in my book
God wants me to go, to really rock and roll with it, not
to wait for my friends to catch up. I've got to go for
God.*

James returned to the UK in March 1992 after a year in
the USA. For him and Simon it was as if they had been
together all the time.

One subject that Simon and James shared a common
interest in was girls. Simon's girlfriends tended to be
much shorter than him. He had a succession of girlfriends

who were infatuated with him. Often he'd pretend he didn't really notice them.

Whenever Simon liked a girl it was a case of just being friends at first. Often a girl would spend many hours with him and then declare her undying love for Simon. He'd be absolutely gobsmacked and never see them again. He got very friendly with girls.

'There was a sweet innocence in Simon's relationship with girls,' James recalled later. 'He was so mature for his age. But when it came to girls, he was as innocent as the average 13-year-old.'

Simon often had intense discussions about boy/girl relationships. He believed strongly that sex before marriage was wrong. But he often debated how far a couple could go. For instance, he'd been brought up with the view that *any* physical contact of a sensual kind—including kissing—was inappropriate until the two people knew they were right for each other. Was this what the Bible *really* meant? In his discussions he'd deliberately swing from one extreme to another in an effort to draw out the other person's viewpoint on the matter.

When it came to his actual relationships with girls, however, sometimes his theory went a bit out of the window. He'd tell James about his struggles to get things right and the two of them would pray for God's wisdom on the matter. James said: 'Simon struggled against entering a physical relationship with a girl. But he knew when to stop and wouldn't have allowed things to go too far.'

Simon wrote concerning his girlfriends:

I love God more than anything in the world and by his grace he always seems to dig me out of the holes I bury myself in.

Sometimes my pride would get so big for itself I'd even try to convince God I was right! But I've learned that prayer doesn't change God's heart; it just gives him access to yours.

God had given me a vision, a purpose in life, an ultimatum. But I'd subconsciously put it on hold and intensified my vulnerability to distractions. That's all I'd done. I just couldn't see it.

I decided with resolute volition I wouldn't get involved with another girl until I found my wife. She would have to have the same vision of where she's going in God and a freedom within herself to express all God's given her. I've met too many people who so want to be free they get caught up in the world's concept of freedom. But earthly freedom can only exist within the laws that define it. Jesus is the only one who can bring complete freedom.

James, too, was beginning to seek his future partner. After a lot of encouragement from Simon, James eventually went out with a girl called Jeanine who worked with him at the same shop in Bath. After a lot of prayer and heartache they fell in love with each other and got engaged. Simon was to be the best man at their wedding on his return to the UK next summer.

Earlier, in October 1992, Simon and James, together with several other young people, decided to put on a special praise event for young people at the Forum, their church building in Bath. The Forum was an old movie house dating back to 1934, renovated in attractive colours and seating up to 1600 people. They got together a dozen quality musicians to lead the praise, including Simon on flute and James on drums. They brought in an acoustics company to provide a massive public address system. They also sent posters round to all the churches in Bath inviting young people to come.

It was a successful event. Hundreds of people showed up. Simon played the flute and James the drums. The praise and worship was really good. Afterwards, James and Simon went round in a complete daze, 'high' on the Holy Spirit. They did a repeat event, then James and the others organised a third one after Simon had left for South Africa.

Around the same time Simon Harrison and the Christian student group put on a student meal for all freshers at the university. There were about 40 or 50 freshers in Simon Harrison's front room. Simon and James each had a circle of students around them and they were being completely stupid. They entertained them for the whole afternoon. It just seemed to happen.

Simon and James loved films, especially wacky ones. When *Wayne's World* came out while they were at the Bible Week everyone who went to see it came back and said to Simon and James, 'You've got to go see this film.

It's all about you.' James's fiancée thought the two were actually funnier than the film.

On Saturday 27 February 1993, shortly before Simon left for South Africa, Simon and James jointly arranged a *Wayne's World* party.

'*It's James' birthday . . . excellent!*' read the invitation. '*Simon's leaving. Excellent . . .not! Come as Garth, Wayne or a babe. Guys, bring a bottle and a babe. Girls, bring a bottle and a Garth or a Wayne.*'

At the party James was the straight dude Wayne and Simon was Garth, the real geeky one. Simon wore a baseball cap that had a blond ponytail hanging from it. They used expressions from the film such as, 'She's a babe.' They talked about 'Babe-raham Lincoln' and 'Babe-alonia'.

The party was held in the basement of the Forum. People of all ages came along. The older generation hated the music but loved the party. The younger generation loved the wild craziness.

James recalled after Simon left for South Africa:

I take after my dad, who is serious and then can be really crazy. I guess that was like me when I was with Simon. Sometimes, though, Simon didn't know when to stop. The trouble was, no one could stop Simon once he'd started.

I'm bolder when it comes to speaking about Jesus. When I was with Simon I had no choice. He and I got to the point where we were indifferent to people's reaction. If they didn't like us for what we believed in, it was their tough luck, 'cos we thought we were cool.

18

Keeping watch

By the time Simon arrived by ambulance at Tygerberg Hospital, Cape Town, at just after 2.00 pm, he had lost consciousness. Not only that, but somehow since the accident, his new watch, which he'd bought with money his parents had given him for his 21st birthday, had gone missing, presumed stolen.

He was given an X-ray of the spine and a brain scan to check for brain damage. Everything was normal. (Sarah, his older sister, commented later that for Simon to have a 'normal' brain scan was a miracle in itself!)

Deon Briedenhann spoke with the hospital on the phone that afternoon after finding out about the accident.

'Should I contact Simon's parents in England?' Deon asked the doctor.

'No, I don't think it's necessary to contact relatives at this stage. I believe we'll be able to see him through.'

Deon and Cedric, both leaders of the church in Somerset West, hurried over to the hospital and managed to find their way into the intensive care unit. This was normally forbidden to all but close relatives.

While Simon lay unconscious, connected up to an assortment of machines and monitors, they prayed for him. They wanted to lay hands on his head as they prayed, but from where they stood they only managed to hold Simon's feet. Simon would have enjoyed the fun of bending the rules in order to pray!

Deon felt at the time that Simon, though in a coma, somehow knew they were there. Eventually, Deon and Cedric were asked to leave.

That night things took a turn for the worse. A test for lung damage showed a measure of deterioration. Simon was transferred to the intensive care lung unit, where it was found that his lungs were filling up with liquid. They put him on a lung machine and decided to contact relatives in the morning.

A friend who knew that Simon was in a coma said, 'I had a vision in which I saw Simon lying on a bed and down each side of the bed were angels. It was like an assignment of angels who worked together. They were singing with heads lifted up. It was as if the air around became music.

'Simon was lying on the bed and he began to sing, *"O how I love the Saviour's name, O how I love the Saviour's name"*, over and over.

'He wasn't looking at the angels but beyond them. I knew he was looking where I couldn't see, and seeing what I've never seen. He seemed very alert but totally oblivious to where he was lying and to his surroundings. He was powerfully drawn to where he was gazing.'

Simon often saw things others couldn't. His long-awaited return to South Africa was the fulfilment of a vision in which he had to take risks in order to help bring justice to situations where injustice still reigned supreme.

19

Nkosi Sikelele Afrika!

Simon's first trip to South Africa in September 1990 was the culmination of a number of messages people brought to him over the previous three and a half years. Simon had kept a careful record of these messages from God, or prophecies, that people had brought him:

March 1987
God sees you as a rock, a foundation, and will use this foundation to build on and to reach out to others. God sees you as someone who hears him and is bold, someone who sticks to what he believes.

November 1987
Don't linger for those who don't want to go on with God, but press on yourself. Don't be afraid to set the trend. Others will follow you. Those who don't will be left behind.

February 1988
God has given you wisdom for other Christians and those outside the Christian community. Walk humbly, using your wisdom to bring life into situations. Use this gift to share it with others, not to let it frustrate you.

February 1988
You are a tall man and God sees you as a skyscraper among other smaller buildings. You are tall in your walk with him and also in wisdom. He wants you to use your spiritual height to see things others can't see and to share with them what he tells you.

The training is over. Now it's time to move on. Let God work through you, stretch out your hand and move forward. The days ahead aren't going to be easy. You will have responsibilities. God is pleased with how you have walked with him so far. It's now time for you to act even in my training.

Pray, speak and bring what God tells you. He says it's *not* time for you to stop learning from your dad. He will teach you many more things. Don't pass over lightly what your dad has to say to you.

November 1988
You are tall physically and spiritually. You can see over other people's heads. You can see the way out of problems. You can see things nobody else can see. God will show you things about others, but you must keep open to what he has to say.

July 1989
God has made you a stirrer of situations. You are to be bold as you go into situations and speak out his word. He is going to use you in amazing ways.

June 1990
God has given you hands to heal and you will see many people healed by the power of God working through those hands.

After his first visit to South Africa Simon had a further prophecy:

December 1991
Don't keep digging into things you're not sure of and don't understand, but rather build on the things God's made you sure of.

God will use you more as you stand firm and don't compromise or move from what he has called you to. He will never, ever leave you. He is always there with you. God's going to use you in ways you couldn't imagine. Don't look to your own understanding, but look to God.

That first trip to South Africa was a real eye opener for Simon. Suddenly, all the talk in Britain of the hated apartheid system, of boycotting Cape apples and of Nelson Mandela's release from prison after 27 years began to come together like pieces of a jigsaw puzzle.

Apartheid. The very word got Simon hot under the collar. Although it had been devised by the early Dutch settlers, apartheid came very much to the fore when Hendrik Frensch Verwoerd, an ardent segregationist, became prime minister in 1958. The master plan that had been evolving in his mind would in future be enforced by law.

Verwoerd's first measure was the 1959 Promotion of Bantu Self Government Bill. This provided for the founding of eight 'Bantu' (non-white) national homelands, with the Minister of Bantu Affairs retaining the right to approve all appointments of chiefs and head men and to veto their decisions. Verwoerd also considered it essential to remove all black representatives from Parliament.

Such reforms had unexpected effects. Many white students supported the blacks in their protests, something new in South African history.

In 1963 Verwoerd established the first homeland government. He encouraged white businessmen to open factories on 'white' land close to the borders of the homelands, bringing jobs to the homelands without diminishing the blacks' autonomy inside them.

Improving the reserves was, however, never a serious priority for the government. They remained populated by more people than they could feed, and they were so over-farmed that the fertility of their land was declining.

The Secretary for Bantu Administration and Development said that those blacks who 'are financially in a position to bear the cost of staying there should be moved into homeland townships with full services'. These were so the blacks employed in the white South African border areas could travel daily to work.

He also said: 'Normally only a rudimentary layout on the basis of agricultural residential areas is undertaken and the delimitation need not be carried out by a surveyor.' Truckloads of Africans, in short, were to be dumped on open ground.

Verwoerd also made it a criminal offence for a non-white student to register at an open university without the written consent of the Minister of Internal Affairs. New universities were founded to make up for the exclusion of non-whites from existing universities. But sending African students to all-black universities—the Africans called them 'tribal colleges'—created a hothouse for new growth, a movement called black consciousness.

During his first visit to South Africa Simon had deliberately gone out of his way to visit the various homelands. Although he had stayed mainly with white Afrikaners who were committed to equality, he had also been into the townships and squatter camps where non-whites lived, often in atrocious conditions. While he admitted that there were no easy answers, he fully supported the end of injustices in South Africa.

Black resistance had begun soon after the first Dutch settlers arrived. In the 1880s, the black people began forming political organisations to seek their rights. In 1902, the South African Native Congress was founded in the eastern Cape. This later became the African National Congress (ANC).

The ANC became more militant after the Bulhoek Massacre of 1921, when a community of African (black) people refused to move from the land they had occupied at Bulhoek, near Queenstown, in defiance of racial zoning. As a result of their protest, 163 people were shot and killed when they charged at the police patrol sent to evict them.

The last desperate attempt by Africans to head off the institution of full apartheid was a series of huge demonstrations and marches in 1948. The new government responded with violence, and hundreds were killed.

Africans were becoming increasingly frustrated with a government determined to extend apartheid. Some members of the ANC, impatient with what they called the excessive caution of their elders, broke away and formed the Pan Africanist Congress (PAC) under Robert Sobukwe.

Both the ANC and the PAC were united in opposing racist remarks by the white extremists. A classic example was: 'We Afrikaners are not the work of man, but a creation of God. It is to us that millions of semi-barbarous blacks look for guidance, justice and the Christian way of life.'

The African people particularly objected to the pass laws, which required them to carry passbooks in order to work in white areas. On 6 April 1952 leaders of the ANC in Johannesburg called for 10,000 volunteers to defy the law of apartheid by leaving their passbooks at home. Theirs was a peaceful protest. 'No violence, no resistance to arrest. *Nkosi Sikelele Afrika!'*

Nelson Mandela, the ANC's Youth League president, was among those arrested without violence or resistance on 26 June 1952. The peaceful protests, including public burning of the passbooks, continued for the next eight years.

Things reached a head on 21 March 1960 when thousands of Africans around the country left their passbooks at home and marched on police stations to demand arrest. It was a non-violent protest but for the 3000 Africans who marched on Sharpeville police station it was soon to become a nightmare. Police opened fire, leaving 67 African people shot dead and 186 wounded, many shot in the back as they fled.

As a result of Sharpeville the ANC and the PAC both formed military wings and decided to use military muscle in pursuing their aims. The ANC created *Umkhonto we Sizwe* (Spear of the Nation) and the PAC created *Poqo* (We Alone). Both went underground at home but set up external missions abroad.

After several prolonged trials, in 1963 Nelson Mandela was imprisoned in Robben Island maximum security prison off the coast of Cape Town.

For years after Mandela's imprisonment, much of the ANC's energies went into the establishment of training camps for guerrillas in several African countries in preparation for the first phases of the armed struggle. The initial phase ordered by Mandela was to sabotage inanimate objects and symbols of minority rule. But if the white minority refused to move, attack was to be shifted to military and police personnel. And should this fail to move whites to negotiate with the African majority, a full scale civil war would be declared.

When Mandela was finally released from Victor Verster prison on 11 February 1990 things had changed considerably. He had spent 27 years in prison, 19 of them on Robben Island. Now Mandela wanted to work towards peace and majority rule.

Simon saw that even Mandela's efforts didn't have all the answers to the needs of South Africa:

People ask me what I think is the answer for South Africa. Well, it always makes me laugh when people's response to a tricky situation is, 'God's the only answer.' This, of course, is true. But it's also a pretty grim excuse for not having to think about it. We have the mind of Christ. Therefore, we have the capacity to answer these problems with practical wisdom involving action.

The Bible says, 'Faith is the assurance of things hoped for.' This is what's going to happen in South Africa. The church of God will grow in its recognition of God's desire for his people to be of one heart in this final age. It will be a people not striving to survive in a multicultural or multiracial society, but rather a racially integrated kingdom with one culture that dedicates itself to making the kingdoms of this world become the kingdom of our God.

God has a history of turning situations around in order that his power is revealed. No earthly power will ever bring peace to South Africa. The eyes of the world are all on South Africa at the moment, and Satan loves it. But God is raising up his church in the middle of it all and it's going to knock Satan right off the map.

The whole world will see the peace and justice of God in his people, a people preparing themselves for his return.

During Simon's six-month visit to South Africa he identified strongly with the black consciousness movement. Sometimes, just to make a point, he'd shout out in the Xhosa language such slogans such as '*Amandla!*' (black power) and '*Awethu!*' (power to the people). One time he hitched a ride in a truck with a white driver. When he was going past some houses he undid the window and shouted, '*Amandla!*'

The white truck driver thumped him!

Simon's concern for Africa went back to when he was a little boy. On 15 January 1986 he wrote:

When I was eight I started collecting Matchbox cars. After several months I had collected ten new and shiny cars. I was really proud of them! Then a man called Nick Wafula from Africa came to stay with us. I felt sorry for his boys, who were back in Africa, so I gave him all my cars to give to his boys. Now, five years later, God is still blessing me with more cars. I have over 100. Thank you, Jesus.

Not all Simon's childhood adventures could be repeated in South Africa. As a child in Bath he had once spent the night sleeping under the stars in a field with his family. All seven of them climbed into their sleeping bags on a groundsheet and lay there looking at constellations and shooting stars. The adventure was part of the regular 'family fun' times the Reynolds family enjoyed. Other family fun times included sleeping under the dining room table—joined by the dog and cat—going rowing and playing rounders in the local park.

Simon and his friend Pete Stevens spent a night sleeping under the stars on the roadside in South Africa and were severely rebuked by a South African who knew how dangerous a place South Africa could be at night.

That first trip to South Africa was part of the fulfilment of Simon's lifelong desire to travel overseas and to be involved in helping people. For part of his time he stayed with Mark and Avril Bird and their four children, Doug, Joanna, Ruth and Stephen.

Mark and Avril were concerned about Doug. Simon kept assuring them that everything would be OK. Doug was merely growing up. 'Just relax,' he'd tell them.

They felt overwhelmed by Doug's mood swings but Simon, being from a large family, knew exactly what Doug was going through. Simon helped to put things in perspective. Kids could stick to God's principles in a distorted world without having to kick over the traces and rebel. They felt that in talking to them about their son, Simon spoke with a wisdom greater than his age.

Joanna, Ruth and little Stephen really took to Simon. Ruth faithfully spilt coffee down him when she took a cup to him in the morning!

Christmas 1990 came round, and with it came the memories of childhood Christmases back home in England. Each year had been different. Instead of a roast dinner his parents often put on a full Indian meal with all the trimmings. One year the children elected to have a picnic of chicken and chips followed by chocolate yoghurt on a tablecloth on the sitting room floor.

Simon had enjoyed Christmas 'open home' for people from their church and other friends. When he was six they had 30 people for lunch and 60 for supper on Christmas day. They all played sardines. After that, they decided to use their church so they could have more room. They moved lamps, rugs and Christmas cards there to make it into 'their' sitting room. The family wore slippers and pretended they were at home.

Simon enjoyed those times, helping to get things ready and welcoming those who otherwise would have had a lonely time. One Christmas all the children slept in one room, leaving bed spaces for people on shift duty who couldn't get home to their families. Another year they had students from eight different nationalities.

When Simon was 16, he and his dad scoured the streets looking for a homeless friend of his called John. They eventually tracked him down but he refused to come for Christmas dinner, which left Simon very disappointed.

For much of that first time in South Africa Simon worked at Bizweni, a former colonial farm set in Somerset West, overlooked by magnificent mountains and lush greenery. Bizweni had been bought by a church and was in the process of being redeveloped for use as a training centre, church, school and nursery.

Bizweni had been used in recent years by local farms producing Cape apples. The same buildings once used for storing and packing apples were now being developed for youth work across the cultures, nursery education and an auditorium to seat 500 people. The old colonial-type houses were being renovated to provide offices.

Sally Jackson was a teacher in the nursery school at Bizweni. She'd gone to South Africa for six and a half months as part of a year out between her A levels and a degree course. She'd heard about Simon as this hard working fellow Brit who'd been in South Africa quite a time. She imagined a small, anaemic looking man. When she finally met him, she felt dwarfed by his size.

In many ways they were opposites. In others they shared things in common. they had both come to South Africa to serve God. For Sally it was potty training seven two-year-olds. For Simon it was building desks for the children.

'Simon was a radical and all out for God,' recalled Sally. 'He wasn't a typical Christian bloke. He had his own views about issues, some of which were contentious. He really was challenging. I hope I was, too. He told me all the dos and don'ts. He'd been in Africa three months already and shared all his mistakes and experiences.'

One of their common goals was to encourage white young people to go along to the mainly Coloured youth group. It was a real challenge. They didn't totally crack the problem but at least they made a dent.

Sally remembered the misunderstandings:

Because we were both from the UK and a similar age, the matchmakers (found at every church, I think) thought it would be lovely if we ended up together, perhaps staying permanently at Bizweni. A lady from the Coloured community invited Simon and me around for a meal. She's a fantastic lady who lives in the Strand in a Coloured township.

Typically she had an enormous family, probably four generations under one little roof. Her husband, a fisherman, went out to sea one morning and never returned. The weather was atrocious, so he was presumed dead.

Simon and I innocently went along thinking it would be a good chance to get to know her better and meet some of her family. We stepped in to find a lovely candlelit, beautifully presented table for two. No single red rose or violinist, but a set-up was smelled in the air. Simon and I sat down and looked at each other knowingly.

Simon asked in a diplomatic way where the family were. They were all in the kitchen cooking, ready to wait on us and make it a really memorable evening for the two of us. We pleaded for her and the family to join us. The thought of taking over their whole living area for the evening was too embarrassing. But they insisted. They were on a mission to see something happen that night.

As usual we had a laugh and chatted a while. Finally, we persuaded our friend to join us and introduce the rest of the family. Once they were all in and talking, there was no stopping them. We had an excellent time.

For his last month or so at Bizweni Simon lived with Clive and Karen. Their house was some distance from Bizweni so he used an old motorbike, the wind-up version with no ignition. Sally thought he looked so funny on it, legs everywhere. But it was a lot quicker than riding Sally's bike.

When Simon left for England the youth put on a surprise braai *(barbecue)*. He was dragged kicking and screaming by a group of girls (actually he loved all the attention), plastered with everything they could lay their hands on (make-up, shaving foam, etc). I admired his courage. He was definitely game for a laugh.

Two people had speeches, all good stuff, saying how he'd made an impact and how they were looking forward to his return. Then they all sang to him:

Friends are friends for ever,
If the Lord is Lord of them,
And a friend will not say, 'Never,'
Because the love will never end.
Though it's hard to let you go,
In our Father's hands we know
That a lifetime's not too long
To live as friends.

A few of us went to the airport and sat with coffee and biccies, chatting about things while waiting for the plane.

Simon suddenly stood on his chair and announced at the top of his voice to the whole airport, 'Ladies and Gentlemen, my time in South Africa has come to an end. I love your country. Thank you for having me. I'll be back. Goodbye!'

The rest of us were dying with embarrassment. Typical. He was unconventional right down to the last detail of getting his flight home. Even though the flight company were calling out his name, he had to finish all his coffee first before he boarded the plane. Ultra casual!

20

Ready to return

When Simon returned to England he was, in many ways, a different person. His experiences in South Africa had matured him. His exposure to injustice had made him more sensitive than ever to the injustices in the world around him. Now more than ever he'd fill his bedroom walls with pictures of hurting people from around the world.

Above all, Simon loved his family, despite the way he'd treated them when he was in his teens. They were cool.

His dad meant a lot to him. He looked up to his dad as his natural father and spiritual mentor. Even while he was in South Africa he'd checked his decisions with Dad when his parents phoned from England. It was a relationship that made others in South Africa envious.

His mum was a person he could confide in. She had always been approachable and he was proud of her.

Sarah and Susie were pretty neat, considering they were sisters. And his relationship with his kid brother Joff was great.

Then there was his other brother, Daniel. They'd had their differences many times. Now Daniel had recommitted his life to Jesus, but what was really great was that Daniel was still cool; he hadn't become stuck in a rut like so many of the church people Simon knew.

Simon's vision for returning to live in South Africa grew over the coming months. When Sally Jackson returned after her extended stay at Bizweni the two of them met and shared snippets of news about people they knew in South Africa. They both yearned to go back.

Simon's sense of fun meant that his communications with people in South Africa were unconventional to say the least. He'd use the fax machine at work to contact old friends in South Africa such as Peter van Niekerk. Once he phoned Peter from a broken phone box from which he could speak without paying. The conversation was only stopped when the telephone repair people came along!

He once wrote to Peter: 'It's 2.30 pm and I've just got home. My boss sent me home because he thinks I'm ill. I'm not; I'm just tired. Oh, well. at least I get paid for it!'

He really missed the four Bird children in Durban where he'd stayed:

So, Dougy, how's it going? Is it this January you're supposed to start boarding school? I should stick with the Huckleberry Finn idea if I were you. You pick up more girls that way. Kids your age that I know would rather take a demented goat to the movies than be seen with a girl.

And how are you, Ruth? Since I left, have you found anyone else's eyes to pluck out first thing in the morning? You could always try your dad. I'm sure he'd really appreciate that.

How about you, Joanna? Do you miss having someone to throw coffee all over to wake them up? I've heard of a bucket of cold water in the face to wake you up in the mornings. But coffee?! Gee wizz, it's like being woken by a team of psychomaniacs.

And Stephen, I don't know if I ever got a chance to tell you: I'm not a trampoline. It's one thing to jump on me while you're awake, but while asleep and lying on my back, to jump on me is to risk ruining my plans for a future family.

Avril, I think you must be the only sane person in the entire family. How did you survive so long? I really do miss you all, though.

I miss packing up the truck and the bakkie *at some ridiculous hour and then driving like psychopathic baboons with a death wish to a market that's closed anyway. I miss dogs with dumb names like 'Ice Cream'. I miss driving tractor mowers through flower beds— sorry about that, Avril—then desperately fighting the temptation and curiosity of wondering whether or not the lawn mower could swim.*

My mum's cutting my hair in a minute. By the way, I've grown my hair at the back and it's in a pony tail. If this affects my request of coming to work for you, then

. . . well . . . tough. The only haircut recorded in the
Bible (Samson), the guy went blind and lost his
relationship with God!

One time Simon wrote to a friend in South Africa about
what God had taught him at a recent Bible week:

God told me to get a small group of young ones
together and start to let God use James and me to
impart some of the things he's taught us over the
years. James is all for it!

Since then God's been showing me again about
purity, holiness and how I should be relating to the
unsaved friends around me.

Jesus calls us the 'salt of the earth' (Matthew 5:13).
Salt melts whatever's frozen: hearts or churches. Salt
preserves what is worth preserving: authentic
Christianity, not some cloistered, monastic aberration.
Salt gives Christianity taste.

It's almost as if we Christians are the 'spice of life'.
Salt makes people thirsty for the living water—Jesus
Christ.

Jesus also calls us the 'light of the world'. Light
dispels darkness. It warms what is cold and can even
melt what is frozen. As light we should be attracting
people to the source of the light, 'the Father of the
heavenly lights' (James 1:17), to reveal God's beauty to
a fallen world.

In October 1992, in preparation for his return trip,
Simon finally plucked up the courage to phone the South
African embassy in London. He'd been scared to phone
and ask for a visa. A person had only one chance to
appeal. If the embassy were to turn down the appeal he'd
have to wait three years to apply again. Simon wrote:

I was put through to three different extensions before I
reached someone who could take the call. He was an
Afrikaner. He asked questions like, 'How much are you
earning? How much money will you take there? Who
are you going to work for in South Africa? How long
are you going for?'

I told him it was under the supervision of a church.
At the end of the phone there was a pause and he

lightened his tone and asked, 'Were you doing this sort of work the last time you went?'

I said, 'Yes.'

Then he asked, 'You don't happen to know Dave Phillips in Durban, do you?'

I couldn't believe it. 'Yes,' I said.

'What about Peter van Niekerk?'

I told him I'd stayed with Peter several times and he was responsible for me on my last trip. To cut a long phone call short, he knew them both well and was himself a Christian. He agreed to send his personal card with my application form. He said, 'Whenever you call the embassy, ask for me and I'll make sure everything runs smoothly.'

Praise God.

As a result of the phone call Simon was given a three-year work permit for South Africa. The final piece of the jigsaw puzzle had fallen into place.

Christmas 1992 came round, the last Christmas Simon was to have with his family before returning to South Africa. Simon didn't have enough money to buy his family any Christmas presents. Instead, he sent each member of his family a poem:

Greetings to all who live under this roof,
And may each of your lives bring eternal youth.
However, this note bringeth bad news,
And tells of a man whose money was misused.

He wined, he dined,
He spent, he lent.
His money as good as down the drain.
He wined, he dined,
He spent, he lent.
He drove his mother quite insane.

The reason for this poetry
Is plain for all to see.
The author is a crafty goose
And simply looking for excuse.
He can't afford a gift to give,
And is begging you to let him live!
So please hold off from shooting him here;

You'll get your 'preseys' in the new year.

They were so enthusiastic about the poem that he got away with it. Despite the promise, his parents, brothers and sisters never did get their presents!

The day before leaving, Simon and his family went to Sydney Gardens, Bath, for a series of family photos. Then the brothers and sisters stood on a park bench like they'd done when they were children. This time passers-by must have thought it strange to see five young people standing on a park bench with a 6'7" giant towering over the other four.

That evening the Reynolds had a family farewell dinner. They prayed together and said their goodbyes. The whole family felt the impact of his leaving. Would they ever see him again?

Then, on Monday 8 March 1993, Dad, Mum and Joff, together with Simon's best friend, James, went to Heathrow Airport to see Simon off.

Soon after that Simon was on the plane bound for the land of his vision, South Africa.

21

No fear!

After his six months' visit to South Africa two years before, Simon knew something of what he was letting himself in for. His desire and call from God first and foremost was to work in the black and Coloured townships and squatter camps.

He wrote to his family back home in England:

Pray that I stay firmly rooted in God's Word and that every decision I make bears clearly within it the hallmarks of the wisdom of God.

Nathan Luckcock wrote to Simon in South Africa urging him not to be a martyr. On 6 July 1993 he replied:

You joked about my being a martyr. I may be big and crazy, but I'm actually a big softy. I'm scared of lots of silly things like spiders, dogs, bees and sharks. But God has barred all fear of township violence from me. It's the weirdest thing. South Africa for me as far as I know is a temporary situation. But I'll give everything I've got to see people saved.

Simon had originally planned to spend two years in South Africa, the first year among Coloured young people and in squatter camps near Cape Town and the second on a project in the Durban area. Because the work was mainly voluntary he planned to work two or three evenings a week to earn some spending money.

As it turned out, when Simon arrived in Somerset West Peter van Niekerk told him that the project in Durban might not be ready in time. He advised Simon instead to go and see the Gateway Project in Pietermaritzburg at the end of his first year.

Brian Andrews, the church pastor, was co-ordinating the project. The church had been given a massive unused prison worth R3-4 million. They were making it into a place for the homeless, alcoholics and the uneducated. It was a scheme to give people a chance in life who didn't have a hope in today's world.

As on his previous visit, Simon got on well with Peter van Niekerk. He loved Peter's unconventional ways and they became good friends.

For his first month in the Cape Simon stayed with a guy called Fred Brown. They got on really well together.

As soon as he could, he sat down with Kobus Swart and another church leader to talk about the year ahead in the Cape. He explained clearly that he wanted to work in townships telling people about Jesus, not being stuck merely doing odd jobs at Bizweni. His first plan was to work in Sun City squatter camp and also Lwandle township.

While the church leaders were happy for him to be involved in work in the townships, they also wanted him to do at least some work at Bizweni. Although Simon was radical, he, too, felt it was important to work within the church context.

He started at Bizweni by making a porch and building furniture for the kids' school.

For a time he worked with a young Coloured guy, Theo Mayekiso, who had just moved down from Transkei. The two would deliver beds to the white community of Somerset West. They were a funny looking pair—fair-haired Simon, white and towering over Theo, the guy from the Coloured community.

Simon enjoyed the stares of people as the two of them worked. He used the difference between them to get across a point. He always referred to Theo as 'Boss' and meekly obeyed whenever Theo gave him an order. Although it was all done as a joke, Theo himself said that the message was clear to white people—apartheid was dead and people of all races were equal. Simon later wrote:

Two power forces are ruling the people here—hatred and fear. Some of all races are burning with hatred, a hatred compelled and driven by a lust for revenge. Others, gripped by the obsessive force of fear, have become victims of irrational compulsion. They have become prisoners within the system that was originally built to maintain their own freedom. But in this world even freedom can only exist within the laws that define it.

Racism in this country has little to do with colour. It's about culture. For example, why do so many even right-wing white South Africans seem to like Eddie Murphy and Witney Houston? Because their cultures are similar to theirs and it shows in their entertainment. Anyone going to South Africa to try to convince black, white, Coloured and Indian people that they're all just the same and must mix together nicely is wasting his time. It's like a blind man in a dark room looking for a black cat that isn't even there.

Sharing the gospel with relevance within a particular cultural context is something we need to learn. Culture is the effect of history, consciousness and destiny on the life of a collective body of people. It's made up of commitments, values and beliefs about the world and the people in it.

Christianity is really the gospel applied in a cultural context involving its expression and a response of the people you're speaking to. Cultural manifestations generally don't contradict or undercut the gospel itself. On the contrary, when functioning properly a cultural Christianity can bring out insights into the gospel that can't be seen in cultural contexts.

Please pray that the Holy Spirit will help me not to limit him to my own cultural values.

One day soon after Simon started working at Bizweni he climbed 20 metres up a tree to cut down some rotten branches. He lost his balance while he was sawing and didn't have a hand free to save himself. 'Fortunately,' as he later described it, his head was big enough to hit a branch before he fell forward enough for his feet to fall off the branch. He ended up with a two-inch diameter graze on his cheek and jarred a nerve in his neck. This led to the most excruciating headache he'd ever known.

By now he was starting to get little presents from home. He'd been sent some chewing gum from his little brother Joff in England and in typical Simon style had given it to some black children at Bizweni. They were so excited about it that they were dancing, singing and going crazy.

He and the young people at Bizweni decided to make a coffee bar for outreach. They found an old barn there that seemed ideal. They got permission to convert it and began the work on it.

Deon Briedenhann, a tall, white English-speaking South African, first noticed Simon while the latter was playing volleyball wearing a red bandanna, cut-off jeans and dark glasses. Deon's immediate impression was that he was a brash, loudmouthed American. Soon, though, they began to get to know each other. Two weeks after arriving in Somerset West, Simon went to stay in Deon's home for a week, which ended up nearly a year.

Thursday 29 July 1993: I've moved in with Deon and Erica and their four-year-old son Matthew Briedenhann. I'm really enjoying staying here. It's five minutes' walk from town (Somerset West) and Bizweni. Deon and Erica lead our cell group, which is quite boring but the others seem to enjoy it. Deon and Erica are great fun and very real. They don't put up with nice Christian talk, so we get on well.

God has been really cool with sorting out friends for me. Everyone remembers me from two years ago. It makes me feel really good. But of course I knew that anyway.

Cell group meetings in Deon's home were always unpredictable thanks to Simon. He was often questioning things. Nothing was left unchallenged. He was eager to learn as much as he could about the Christian life, but he couldn't stand religious nonsense.

Simon and Deon, although 20 years apart in age, hit it off well. They had a kind of kindred thinking, spending long hours talking together in the car. Deon was impressed with the insight Simon seemed to have. He was especially mature in his understanding of relationships. Simon knew, though, that while he could often help others, he found it very difficult to get relationships right for himself.

Deon remembered the story of how a banana once saved Simon's life. Simon was working on some communication poles in a remote spot. He had to go into town in the *bakkie* and noticed a couple of black guys sitting in their car watching him. When he returned and was getting out of the *bakkie*, he saw that the two guys were still in their car and realised they were up to no good.

Simon remembered he had a banana for lunch in the glove compartment. Making sure the guys could see his movements clearly, he leaned back into the cab, reached into the glove compartment and took out the banana. Concealing it in his huge hand, he carefully pocketed his 'weapon'. Suddenly, the car engine roared into life and the two men sped off, scared that Simon would shoot them.

When Deon heard the story he was shocked rigid. Using a banana or anything else to imitate a pistol was highly dangerous. In the violent climate of South Africa Simon could so easily have been shot because of it. But Simon continued to enjoy telling the story, 'How a banana saved my life!'

By now Simon had put on quite a bit of weight. Simon at 6'7" and Deon at 6'5", both fairly hefty, made a formidable pair. Simon enjoyed lining up at the supermarket checkout and picking a mock argument with his 'dad', Deon. The two huge men would be going at each other at the top of their voices, secretly watching the shocked and even fearful stares of the shoppers all around them, just for the fun of it!

Right from the time Simon first arrived at Deon and Erica's he urged them to have a big party. They decided that his 21st birthday in August was the ideal time for a 'major bash', as Simon called it.

With their encouragement Simon invited 50 people from all racial and cultural backgrounds to a sheep roast. A farmer from Karoo supplied a lovely big sheep and Simon got permission to store it in the cold room at the hotel where he worked.

Simon and a couple of friends dragged the tarpaulin-covered sheep through the lobby of the plush hotel to the cold room at the back. Later, he enjoyed seeing the shock on people's faces as he recounted the story. He wrote:

The party was a great success. People are still talking about it now. Many Christians here are quite legalistic in terms of parties, so it was great to crack them open a little. It was a good opportunity to introduce a lot of Christians to fun. Now many are asking when the next one is.

Simon loved people who were outcasts and down-trodden. Nobody was too much of an outcast for him. Once he picked up a six-year-old Coloured boy pushing his little bike late at night. Simon took the lad home and gave him his own bed for the night. It emerged that the boy had left his relatives where he'd been staying and had set out to find his mother.

The following day Simon and Deon took the boy 250 km to where his mother was staying. Only when the little boy was reconciled with his mother was Simon satisfied. The experience was widely recounted, but to Simon it was just one of the things he did to show God's love.

By now Simon had become very much part of the Briedenhann family. Little Matthew really took to Simon. For his part Simon enjoyed teasing Matthew, teaching him tricks and playing games with him.

Simon noticed that Matthew tended to blubber when little things went wrong for him. He decided to help Matthew get over being a 'cry baby'. Every time Matthew cried like that, Simon would call him 'Matilda' (from the poem 'Matilda cried fire, The people all shouted, "Little liar"'). Gradually Matthew got the message that that sort of crying was only for wimps. Simon had helped him to mature during those few months.

Another advantage of living with Deon and Erica was that from time to time Simon managed to get work with Deon's company, Peninsula Poles. The company put up huge masts that picked up radio and car phone signals. The masts had to be painted and maintained regularly.

Simon enjoyed working for Deon. He would drive in a *bakkie* to various parts of South Africa fixing or painting the poles. Some of the poles were 50 metres high. He had to climb a ladder on the inside of them. It was fun work and not too challenging.

His most gruelling experiences, however, were while working as a bouncer at the hotel bar. He had the advantage of being much bigger than the mainly Coloured clientele, so there wasn't as much trouble as there might have been.

When trouble brewed, Simon went into action sometimes before he could think of the consequences. One time there were four guys causing trouble. Simon and the bar owner easily sorted them out and phoned the police. Then they watched in amusement as a whole gang of police couldn't get the four lads into the police van!

To keep himself fit for his nightclub duties Simon worked out in a gym for two hours at a time, three days a week.

Simon continued to visit as many townships as he could. One time he went into the townships with a camera, taking as many photos as possible. The following week, once the pictures were developed, he travelled with Eben Louw, a young Christian guy who acted as his translator into Afrikaans.

They spent most of the day walking through the whole township giving out photos. The people, young and old, were delighted. Their faces creased into grins or they burst out laughing as they recognised themselves and others in the photos. For some people it was the first time they'd seen themselves in a photo.

One of the things that delighted Simon was the way he was able to relate with elderly people. He first got to know 71-year-old Auntie Louisa when he met her in church one Sunday. Simon volunteered with a couple of the other guys to fit a sink for her in her tiny shack in Waterkloof squatter camp, where she lived.

Now that Simon had got to know where Auntie Louisa lived, he visited her once a week, travelling to her humble home in the *bakkie*. He treated her like his own grandmother, cheering her up, talking about the God she loved and trying out on her some of the Afrikaans words he'd learnt that week.

On Sunday afternoons, Simon and a couple from the church would take Auntie Louisa to Sun City, where the four of them would visit poor people.

Simon had been a cautious and fearful child. His grandfather, a well known missionary in South Asia, recalled, 'Simon always looked before he leaped.' But with God's love burning within him, Simon had conquered his fears:

I'm convinced I'm in the right place at the right time and I want to do my part in his plan. I want the ultimate—I want to be like Christ. But if you want the ultimate—you've got to be willing to pay the ultimate price.

I can honestly say that I'm genuinely not afraid to die. It's never tragic to die doing what you love the most. I love serving God, knowing I'm where he wants me and doing what he wants me to do.

Simon's work as a bouncer was becoming more taxing. He was now having to carry a knife for self-defence and he was involved in several serious scuffles.

In mid-November 1993 he had an operation on his hand after having had to use his fist to stop a drunkard who was out of control. He went to a government hospital, which was very basic and mostly non-white. He wrote to his parents about the experience:

Having never had an operation or been under general anaesthetic before I was quite nervous anyway; when the doctors, who were rushing around all over the place with different patients, asked me which hand they were taking the pins out of, I started getting scared. They were supposed to be putting them in, not taking them out!

They gave me a dopey sort of drug to make me go all sleepy. Then they wheeled my bed through to the operating theatre, where they had one of those huge, round lights above me like they have in the movies.

I was aware of what was going on but couldn't say anything or move. I hated that. Then they took my left hand—the wrong one—and strapped it down to a sort of tray. It was like combining the ultimate in frustration and desperate fear into one emotion that just wanted to explode but somehow couldn't.

I heard a nurse say she was going to give me another injection that would send me to sleep. I felt the needle go in and just didn't have the energy to try anymore to tell them they'd got the wrong hand.

The next thing I remember was waking up in the ward and they'd got the right hand. Phew!

Later I took the bandage off to have a quick peep (though they told me not to). It's a weird feeling to see

*metal bars sticking out of my hand. Please pray for me,
though. The doctors say that, as this is the second time
those two knuckles and that bone have been disturbed,
they might not ever be quite right.*

*My only concern is that it doesn't affect my flute
playing. So, just trust God with me that it comes right.*

Simon often wrote to his parents expressing his concerns and asking for their advice on the way forward. He talked about his whole family with affection, putting a special emphasis on his relationship with his dad. He'd write to Peter or phone him up to ask for his wisdom on a wide range of issues.

Simon stopped working in Sun City because he felt he was cramping the style of the cell group leader working there:

*I feel so obligated to do something spiritual, something
impressive, but I don't have to try to impress God, so
why should I try to impress people?*

*Please pray for me that God will show me practically
the way forward for me here. Township projects are
very limited now in terms of what I can do in them as
violence is increasing unbelievably. There are constant
killings of blacks by blacks, more and more of whites
by blacks in townships. I need to know what God
wants me to do.*

*My heart is here. Not only in South Africa but here in
the Cape, in Somerset West. I know that God wants me
in Bizweni. It's encouraging to know that there are
many others whom God has brought here over the last
year or so who feel exactly the same as me. God's up
to something. He knows what he's doing and it
involves me.*

*I'm not going to feel obligated to do anything
anymore, not like last time I was here. I feel like I'm
learning so much about people, myself, church, the
world, political hatred and all kinds of stuff.*

*Though I hate the term, I know what people mean
when they say they're going through a spiritual
wilderness. I felt I'd lost touch with the reality of the
Holy Spirit for a while a few months back. Since then
I've been gripped with an untiring desire to know who
Jesus Christ really is. I can't go on wondering what he*

*would do if he were in my shoes when I don't know
what he was really like when he walked the earth.
I feel great now. I'm discovering a Jesus I didn't
really know much about before.*

After praying about it, Simon decided the time had
come to quit his work in the hotel bar. After that, his
spare time job was selling ice creams on the beach in
Cape Town. He was totally out of money and was hoping
to earn quite a bit. The schools broke up in mid-
December and ice cream sellers could make between
R600 and R1000 a day. This compared with the average
wage for an unskilled worker of R250-300 a week.

He had good times when he wasn't working. He got on
particularly well with Eugene Sitzer. They would go out
together with two guys called Cyril and Eben. Simon
would have his car stereo at full blast playing something
like Eric Clapton's song, *Would you know my name if I
saw you in heaven?* They were a crazy bunch. At pubs
they would play 'spin the beer bottle', kissing the girls
when the bottle pointed to them.

He was growing increasingly frustrated with church
politics, with people engaged in backbiting and criticising
others, as well as with those struggling for positions and
status:

*Titles, flattering as they may sound to our tiny minds,
are merely job descriptions. Positionalism is like a
crippling poison to both church growth and spiritual
growth within the church. Positionalism, the essence of
church politics, will always cripple the spiritual growth
of an individual as it focuses on either oneself or
another man. Hence the focus is taken off God.*

When Simon's church pastor from Bath, Paul Wakely,
visited South Africa he and Simon spent quite a bit of
time together. Simon told Paul about the various jobs he
had done, including working as a bouncer in the hotel
bar. He'd even been offered a job as a debt collector in
Khayalitsha township with two armed men to
accompany him!

Simon was extremely frustrated about the youth work
in the church, which had diminished in size and
importance since he was last in South Africa. He'd

withdrawn from youth work in October since he somehow didn't feel he fitted. He told Paul how instead he wanted to do some work with the young people in a local new township. He was starting afresh by making friends with the people there.

Although youth and township projects hadn't worked out the way Simon had wanted, he told Paul he was still convinced God wanted him in South Africa. He didn't want to go up to Durban until God had established and fulfilled the reason for Simon being there in the Cape.

Paul warned him against settling down to a 'comfortable adventure' mode of living. He encouraged Simon instead to keep a constant awareness of God's call on his life. He could take stock at the end of the first year if no specific opportunities had opened for him.

Paul enjoyed his time with Simon. He found his conversation stimulating and he enjoyed his radical views.

He recalled later:

When Simon first met me at the train station in Cape Town he was three quarters of an hour late, which was unusual for him. Eventually he appeared, limping, his face bruised and wincing with pain. He'd been beaten the night before by five guys using chair legs. But he didn't seem disheartened by it. He was always on the edge of danger, the edge of happenings, and in that sense he was more radical than most Christians.

At the end of our time together I was left with an odd feeling. In my thinking I couldn't seem to fit him in anywhere for the future. It was as if somehow his future on earth had already been mapped out.

22

Early morning shock

The phone shattered the early morning silence with its shrill insistence. Peter Reynolds glanced at his clock—5.40 am. Who could possibly be ringing at this unearthly hour?

It was Kobus Swart, calling from Cape Town.

'I'm sorry to tell you, Peter, your son Simon's had a road accident and is in a coma.'

'Why? What happened?'

He gave Peter the details, then said goodbye.

It was now nearly 24 hours after the accident, yet this was the first the family had known about it. Peter decided to phone the hospital in Cape Town and get the full details from the consultant.

A few minutes later he got through to Dr Smedema at Tygerberg Hospital, Cape Town.

'We've just heard the news about Simon. How bad is he?'

'Not too good, Mr Reynolds.'

'What are the prospects for a full recovery?'

'Well, he has a 50:50 chance of surviving.'

'So is now the time I should be coming out to see him?' Peter asked.

'Yes, I think so,' the doctor replied gloomily.

For the next few minutes Peter was on the phone to various airlines trying to get a flight so he could go to South Africa and be with Simon at the hospital. It was proving difficult because it was so close to Christmas.

Upstairs, Simon's mum, Barbie, lay in bed wondering who could be ringing so early and talking for so long. A special sense of the presence of God filled the bedroom.

Verses from the Psalms ran through her mind: 'He who dwells in the shelter of the Most High will rest in the shadow of the Almighty. 'He is my refuge and my fortress.' The person who fears God 'will have no fear of bad news'.

Cocooned in a blanket of God's love, Barbie knew that whatever the phone call was about, God would be faithful, 'a stronghold in times of trouble'.

Peter told Barbie the news and together they woke Daniel, Susie and Joff. They prayed together for Simon.

Peter phoned friends in the church. There was a system in their church known as a 'prayer chain' so that everyone could be informed quickly if a problem arose that needed prayer. One person would contact a couple of others and they in turn would pass the message on.

Even though it was still early in the morning, by 7.30 am most of the church in Bath had been told of the accident and many were now praying. In Bizweni a 'prayer chain' had been activated the night before.

By 7.35 am Peter had at last booked his flight and had begun getting his things packed ready to leave for the airport. Just before he went out of the door at 8.10 am he strongly felt he needed to call the hospital one more time.

'I'm afraid, Mr Reynolds, I have some bad news,' said Dr Smedema. 'Simon's condition deteriorated and he died 10 minutes ago. I'm so sorry.'

Peter was numbed. Why? How could this have happened? Couldn't anything more have been done?

As the rest of the family at home were told, they went into various states of shock. Several of them had nose bleeds within a few minutes.

Sarah was still recovering from her own son's stillbirth when she had the phone call saying that Simon was in a coma. Susie went straight round to be with Sarah as Dave had already left for a business trip. Then, 10 minutes after she arrived, Susie took the phone call with the news that Simon had died. Susie was absolutely shocked. Sarah, on the other hand, was too numb already.

'I couldn't feel any more than I was already feeling about my baby, Timothy,' she recalled later. 'I was experiencing every form of grief. There weren't any more tears left to cry. At the time it was helpful to the rest of the family, who were in such a state of shock. Heaven seemed so close. It seemed to me that another one had stepped over the threshold into heaven.'

After meeting with Peter's fellow church leader, Paul Wakely, and his wife Sue, Peter and Barbie decided to bury Simon in the Cape rather than fly his body home. It was the least they could do to honour their son, whose vision was to break down barriers in South Africa.

At 10.00 am, less than two hours after hearing news of Simon's death, Peter spoke to his longstanding friend, Christian leader Bryn Jones, who encouraged the whole family to go to South Africa to attend the funeral.

After the family had contacted Dave, Sarah's husband, who was away on a business trip, Bryn, through the help of his secretary, Caroline, managed to arrange a flight to Cape Town the same day for the whole family of seven. That was amazing in itself after Peter's difficulty in getting just one seat for the following day because of the Christmas holiday season. Money for the considerable cost of the fares came from many churches around Britain.

They were due to leave Bath at 2.00 pm that day. One snag was that Daniel's passport was at the Indian embassy in London waiting for a visa. A courier had to be arranged to pick it up and get it to the ticket desk at Heathrow. They were still negotiating its collection on a mobile phone half an hour before they arrived at Heathrow.

Soon, though, the seven Reynolds family members were on their long, sad journey to Cape Town, South Africa.

23

Who will fill these boots?

The Reynolds family arrived in Cape Town on Friday 17 December after a 12-hour flight from England. They were met by two of the church leaders in Somerset West, Deon and Cedric. Peter asked to be taken straight to the hospital where Simon had died.

Dr Smedema was extremely understanding and kind. (It emerged later that he was a committed Christian.) He took them to see Simon's body. Simon seemed larger than ever and looked very peaceful, with just the trace of a smile on his face.

They then went to visit Vally Vallela, who was lying in a hospital bed still recovering from his injuries. Peter, Barbie and the family prayed for Vally and for his wife, who was sitting with him.

Deon took the family back to his home, where they met his wife, Erica. Deon, Erica and Matthew moved out so they could all be together in one house.

Twice a day for the duration of their stay people in the church brought them meals prepared and ready to eat. They were also offered the loan of more cars than they could possibly drive.

Over the next few days a post mortem was carried out on Simon. This put the cause of death down to multiple fractures and 'shocked lung'. There were fractures to his right leg and arm, his collar bone and several ribs. Because of the extent of violent deaths in South Africa, an inquest into Simon's death would have to wait over a year until 1995.

The funeral took place at Hottentots Holland Covenant Community Church in Bizweni, Somerset West. Over 300 people attended the service. They came from different races, colours, beliefs and walks of life. Simon had been in South Africa for just nine months yet had influenced the lives of hundreds of people of all ages.

White Afrikaners and little black Africans from the townships wept together. Many spoke of a young man who was unique, radical in his love for God and caring deeply for other people.

In the front row sat Peter and Barbie Reynolds, together with Simon's two brothers, two sisters and brother-in-law. With them were some of Simon's many friends and work colleagues.

Simon's plain wooden coffin stood at the front. On it sat Simon's huge black, size 13 desert boots, still ponging, still scruffy. In those boots he had carried the message of Jesus Christ to the townships and squatter camps of South Africa.

Also on the coffin was Simon's well used silver flute. Many people had been deeply inspired over the years as he played worship songs so beautifully on that flute. The older generation would remember seeing pictures of the coffin of the great jazz musician, Louis Armstrong, who died aged 71 on 6 July 1971, a year before Simon was born. On Armstrong's coffin was the golden trumpet that had been a symbol of his life. It seemed fitting that Simon, too, should be remembered in this way.

The 'genial young giant of a man', as someone described him, was no longer here. He had been cut off in his prime by a freak road accident a few days before Christmas.

Which of the several tapes he had with him had Simon been listening to before the accident? Was it Bryn Jones preaching on *The Cross?* Or Larry Tomczak on *Looking to the Future?* Or *Perseverance?* Or was it Rick Goodwin on *The Bride of Christ.* Or perhaps it was a music tape. Simon loved music.

Simon had underlined some verses in his Bible, which his mum, Barbie, read out in a version known as *The Message:* 'If I acted crazy, I did it for God; if I acted overly serious, I did it for you. Christ's love has moved me to such extremes. His love has the first and last word in everything we do' (2 Corinthians 5:15).

Another passage of the Bible that Simon had marked in his Bible was: 'We know that when these bodies of ours are taken down like tents and folded away, they will be replaced by resurrection bodies in heaven—God-made, not handmade—and we'll never have to relocate our "tents" again. Sometimes we can hardly wait to move—

and so we cry out in frustration . . . The Spirit of God whets our appetites by giving us a taste of what's ahead. He puts a little of heaven in our hearts so that we'll never settle for less' (2 Corinthians 5:1-5 *The Message*).

Vally—his neck still in a brace as a result of the accident—was there together with his family.

He later recalled the time when he was lying semiconscious on the side of the road. In great pain, he thought he was going to die. Then in a vision he saw Jesus in a beautiful green place with white doves behind him.

'But Jesus didn't like me,' he later told his foreman. 'So he sent me back.'

His foreman, a Christian, explained that it wasn't that Jesus didn't like him but that Vally wasn't ready to meet Jesus. Simon was.

At the end of the funeral service, one girl came forward to receive Jesus Christ as her Lord and Saviour. Others made commitments to God of various sorts.

After the funeral the Reynolds family spent two days with Kobus and Hazel Swart at their home in Hermanus. They visited some of Simon's friends in Sun City. They met Rachel and two of her grandchildren, Gladys and Joyce, as well as Eugene—the ANC local chairman—and some of his family.

During their stay in South Africa the Reynolds family went with Deon and Simon's friend, Fred Brown, on the two-hour journey to the crash site. Part of the crash barrier had been removed in order for the *bakkie* to be towed away. The tyre marks were still clearly visible.

They also visited Piketberg Hospital and spoke with staff and ambulance workers who had taken care of Simon before the long journey to Cape Town.

Finally, on Christmas Eve, they paid one last visit to Simon's as yet unmarked grave. This would later have a headstone with the words 'Loved God, loved people, loved Africa. "Unless a grain of wheat falls to the ground and dies, it remains only a single seed. But if it dies, it produces many seeds"—John 12:24 NIV'.

It would have been good to give away all Simon's clothes to the people in the townships. Unfortunately, most of them were, as usual, threadbare.

Sarah and Dave, still mourning the recent loss of their stillborn baby Timothy David, had mixed emotions in

South Africa. 'I felt guilty crying because of my baby while everyone else was crying for Simon,' recalled Sarah later. 'But I wasn't ready to cope with that just then. I think we'd have felt very differently if the baby hadn't died.

'Looking back to our last phone conversation, I was relieved that Simon had so much to say when we broke the news about the baby to him. It was a shock to hear him saying that England was no longer his home. He lived in South Africa now. I had a week to come to terms with the fact that he was never coming back to England again. I guess it was God's timing to prepare me for his death.'

Exactly a year later, Sarah and Dave became the proud parents of Naomi Joy. While their new baby didn't take Timothy's place, she made a wonderful Christmas present for the whole Reynolds family.

After they arrived back in England, the Reynolds received over 300 letters and cards of tribute from around the world, including Asia, North America, Europe, Africa, New Zealand and the Orient.

A youth fund was set up in honour of Simon to continue his work in South Africa. Within a short time thousands of pounds had been contributed by people from all over the world. This fund continues to grow.

On 3 January 1994, an astonishing 800 people attended the memorial service for Simon's life. The service took place in the Forum, the cinema-turned-church in Bath city centre. They came from all over Britain—north, south, east and west.

The family were amazed to see church leaders from all over Britain, some of whom having travelled hundreds of miles to be there.

At the service, people were reminded of Simon's radical lifestyle. He treated children and adults with the same degree of respect. Children of many different nationalities and backgrounds loved him. Adults were provoked by his radical beliefs and lifestyle. Old people adored him. Young people were challenged by his wild, uncompromising ways.

Bryn and Keri Jones, Christian leaders and longstanding friends of the family, both spoke of a young man who loved God and made an impact with his life.

Keri had had a deep influence on Simon's life from when he was very young. He had visited the family from time to time and was aware of Simon's struggles. Simon had known Keri was praying for him as he grew up. In South Africa recently Keri and Simon had gone for a walk and sat by the roadside. Simon had had lots of questions about God and concerns about the church. Simon had been surprised and relieved that Keri also shared many of his concerns about the church.

Bryn, too, had had an impact on Simon in many ways. When Simon was 20, as people were praying for their Christian leaders at a Bible Week, Bryn called him personally on to the platform in front of thousands of people to pray for his parents.

Bryn said at the memorial service: 'In a short space of time, Simon accomplished more than many people do in their entire lives.'

As a tribute to Simon, Bernard Brooks drew a picture of Simon's boots and flute as they appeared at the front. This was used widely to continue the challenge Simon had issued in his lifetime. Sadly, Bernard died on 25 January 1994, three weeks after the memorial service to Simon. He left a widow, Marjorie.

As at the funeral service, people gave their lives to Jesus Christ at the memorial service.

Once again Simon's boots and flute were on display at the front. One Christian leader, Mike Godward, was sitting looking at Simon's boots. He had a strong urge to stand up in the middle of the service and say, 'Who will fill these boots?' He didn't do it, but he felt strongly rebuked by God afterwards.

The vision he had had during the service grew in intensity. He saw in a vision (or in his imagination, he wasn't sure) hundreds and hundreds of young people standing up and shouting, '*I* will fill those boots. *I* will fill those boots.'

Since then, in his travels around Britain and Africa, he has met many young people who were at the memorial service and who had been inspired to take up that very challenge. He knew personally of at least seven young people who had gone to work in East and Central Africa as a direct result of Simon's death. Others had written to him to say that they were planning to go out there in the future because of Simon's influence on their lives.

Four months after Simon's death, thousands of people at Spring Harvest, a major Christian convention in Minehead, Somerset, heard Christian leader Wesley Richards read out Simon's poem *Risk* and speak about Simon's radical lifestyle. As a direct result, 300 young people responded to an appeal and came forward, declaring their willingness to serve God around the world.

Already, more people had been deeply inspired by Simon's death than throughout his entire 21 years of life.

24

What he meant to me

We were closer than two brothers, provoking each other spiritually.

I'll always remember in his apartment, Simon sitting on the armchair, me sitting on the other side of the room, just having a drink and talking about anything and everything under the sun. My relationship with Simon was very special. My other friends are different people, and I accept them for who they are.

The things I miss most are Simon's attitude to life, his friendship and the fact that he was trustworthy and would never let me down. I could be completely myself with him.

Because I could only do those crazy things with Simon, people think I've gone totally boring. That's not true. I have to be comfortable to do them. I guess I don't take life quite so seriously and I'm still quite wild and wacky as a result of him.

Simon was due to be best man at my wedding. I was blaming God for letting him die and taking away the only close friend I had apart from my fiancée. Matt Wheeldon stood in for Simon as best man. It seemed as if Matt and I hardly knew each other. In the end, it was great.

Simon was a one-off. He went against many of the social conventions. If he'd lived to get married I could imagine him wearing jeans, a teeshirt and a jumper with holes in it for the big day. He'd do it just to make a point.
James Porter

He wasn't a supersaint or anything like that, but he was very mature in his views. He was a radical who didn't take things at face value but wanted to question everything and come to his own conclusions. He'd have been difficult to accommodate in some churches!

Paul Wakely, a leader of Simon's church in Bath

He continues to be a challenge to me, especially in the area of personal evangelism. His ability to talk so freely about God with anybody is something I want. Simon's flagrant lack of inhibition was contagious.

When we were together, we didn't care if anyone heard us singing. Half of Widcombe must have! We wanted to sing and express the joy we both felt.

Simon reminded me of the *Dead Poet's Society*. We don't know how much time we've got so we need to 'seize the day'.

Nathan Luckock

I was very shattered when I heard that Simon had died. I miss him being around. I miss his warmth and his welcoming ways.

Frances Neale

He was a ringleader and a party animal. It didn't bother him whether a person was young or old, married or single, divorced or a single parent. He made each person feel special and important.

Simon was one of the only people I've ever felt really understood me and where I was coming from. Although at times he appeared to have a tough exterior, inside he was sensitive and caring.

I admired Simon's uncompromising walk with God, his wisdom and his knowledge of God's Word. I don't want to paint a glossy picture of him, because that would be unreal, but he was a godly example to many people, especially to me.

It's often hard to tell a brother or sister how much they mean to you. But I wish I'd told Simon face to face how proud I was that he was my brother and friend. It's always good to spend time with someone you look up to, admire and learn from. Simon was that person to me.

At parties, in church meetings and just walking through town together, I felt so proud of him.

I want Simon's death to count for something in my own life. I want to be sharp in God's Word as he was. I want to know, as Simon did, that everything I do each day of my life is what God wants me to be doing at that time. In that way I, too, will be totally ready for the day I come face to face with Jesus, whenever that might be.

Susie Reynolds, Simon's sister

Simon was very important to me—a special brother. God sent Simon to introduce me to the local church. He meant a lot to me.

When I heard he died, I thought it was a joke. I couldn't believe it. I had a strong feeling that I wanted to cry but I had to keep up the courage. When I was on my own, I cried a lot. I'd never before cried for my friends or even my sisters when they died back at home. I couldn't control myself. Even now I cry sometimes.

Jorge Mabuza

Simon would go out and talk to abusive young people high on drink and drugs. Because he was such an imposing guy and not a wimp, he'd talk about God and they'd listen. There was one young guy who was on the downward spiral. He was desperately upset when he heard about Simon's death. It gave me an opportunity to talk about why Simon had gone to South Africa.

Diana Musters

It took a long time for Simon's death to sink in. We all have only a certain amount of time on earth. The way Simon lived his life was such an example to other people. It's given people a lead into talking about God.

I was very sad when it happened, but I felt peaceful about it. It was like Simon was ready. He'd come in, done what he was supposed to do and then gone to be with God. Each of us has a script; many of us stray from that, but Simon followed it to the letter.

Andy Theaker

I made a collage of Simon's poem *Risk*. The collage was a way of sharing with my family how I knew Simon.

He once got us all invited to the hotel bar in Cape Town for an evening on the house. As hungry travellers we pigged out and Simon introduced us to all the weird and wonderful friends he'd made there while working as a bouncer.

That was one thing about Simon. He had a real gift of befriending people. He could relate to and befriend anybody and everybody, influencing them for Jesus, no matter what situation, class or culture. I was one of those he befriended and I knew with Simon I'd be a friend for life.

He was wild, fun to be with, loved life and lived it to the full. But more important, he was someone who had a real sense of God's commission for his life. He wanted to share Jesus with everybody and have a very real relationship with his Lord. He fell in love with South Africa and its people.

I look forward to seeing Simon again when we all get together in heaven, our true home with Jesus, but I realise I'll probably have to wait in one long queue.

Sally Jackson

We really miss our friend, especially his unreligious approach to life, which he displayed in such a humorous way, causing a strong bond to develop between us.

His life spoke volumes, especially in the pubs, places where most Christians fear to tread. It was Simon's belief that God was busy raising his young people to move out of the pews and into the world. As he once said: 'Salt melts what is hard. It adds spice to life.'

He had a strong sense of God's calling on his life. After everyone had left the men's camp, the three of us stayed on and discussed our mutual feelings of frustration concerning what God expected of us. But Simon concluded in his wise way that one can't hear from God until you're relaxed and have made peace with where you're at.

A mere three weeks before his death he experienced this peace, saying he relaxed in the knowledge that God had a plan for him. We really marvelled at this 21-year-old's wisdom. We always listened to what he had to say. Deep inside we were in agreement as if we clicked inside.

Simon had so much wisdom to impart. He was always bored with basic Christian doctrine. He wanted to go deeper. He wanted to teach others more new and unheard of things about God. We thrashed out together controversial issues that were often ignored in Christian circles.

He was very unorthodox. We found this refreshing. It drew people to Simon like a magnet. His lack of religiosity was replaced by a real, honest and remarkable relationship with God. This shone through even to those blind eyes in the pubs who just knew there was something special about Simon.

Anyone could relate to him. His versatility made a witness far louder than any of us could be. His witness was without prejudice of any race, colour or even language. People liked this about him. Where they may have disagreed with him sometimes, they nevertheless stuck with him.

Simon would never reject anyone. His compassion for people, his desire to introduce them to Christ, outweighed any differences there might have been. We truly admired this freedom Simon had to befriend people of all races, from all walks of life.

Fred was impressed by Simon's lack of male chauvinism. He was very honest with women, uninterested in any relationship that was frivolous and not ordained by God. He was determined to walk a straight and pure path.

Simon was unaware of God's plan for him to die. He believed that we should not submit to death but actively resist it. God instructs us to work together actively with his will. We believe Simon would have chosen life because he knew he could be productive and contribute to God's work. He wanted to fulfil his task on earth. This was very important to him. Little did he know that his task would be completed in death.

One of the first questions I asked having heard about his accident was, 'Why, if it was God's plan for Simon to die, did he allow those hours of coma to pass giving many of us the hope of his healing? It then came to me that in those hours God and Simon could have been engaged in conversation as though they were sorting out a couple of things. Maybe God even gave Simon the option to return to us, letting Simon decide whether he wanted to die, and he then chose to be with God. This wouldn't be surprising, for Simon really loved God.

Fred lost another friend of his two days after Simon's death. In a short period of time Simon influenced and touched the lives of far more people than this girl who had been living all her life in South Africa. His testimony was far greater as a true son of God.

Just the way people handled the deaths of these two people. In Simon's case there was a God-given strength that eased the pain. We all found security in the knowledge that Simon was with his Father. In the girl's funeral people were left confused and uncertain, unable to understand the purpose of God. As Mel Clements told us, 'When Simon died, I saw Jesus rejoicing because his child was finally with him.'

He was like a partner in crime (good crime!). Nothing we did together was conventional. We went upstream, challenging tradition, constantly questioning and analysing what most Christians blindly took for granted. It was so much fun serving God this way with Simon (and Fred). It turned our Christian walk from a boring one to a truly spicy one.

Reflecting on our last few months with Simon, it feels as though God gave us a gift, one that brought much joy. Then God suddenly took it back. We miss him but rejoice in the thought of him happy and fulfilled with God.

I think of Simon as upright, serious about God yet so light in his approach to life, always seeking to live righteously, yet in such an unconventional manner. He was a free thinker who lived freely, yet he never allowed his freedom to cross godly boundaries. I really admired this combination of wildness/liberty and unquestioning submission to God's rule in his life.

Simon had only one face—it didn't change in or out of church. This made him a trusted source for wisdom and understanding about life in general and God and religion.

There were no twists and turns, hypocrisy or deceit, about him. What you saw was what you got. What he said was what he honestly believed and lived. One face, one chosen path, one witness, one friend who was available to everyone without discrimination.

I thoroughly enjoyed Simon's company. When he spoke I wanted to listen; when he partied I wanted to join in. He was the life and soul of our little parties and a big bonding factor. Simon broke the ice, opened the doors and showed us all that life in Christ is really great.

He left a deep mark on my heart just like when cattle

get branded with an iron that's been heated in the fire. I know God placed Simon here for a purpose. My friendship with him left me changed in many ways.
Zerélda Swart and Fred Brown, two of Simon's friends

I work from home. When Simon died all my motivation for working went that day. I'll always remember where I went. I work in crop protection and I spend much of my time walking the crops. I went to this lovely valley with a stream running through it and I went walking there. I couldn't face meeting and talking with people.

Because he went to South Africa I found it more difficult to believe that he was dead. Perhaps that was a blessing in disguise.
John Porter

Simon really loved God, loved people and loved life. I'm proud to have been his brother.
Joff Reynolds, Simon's brother

Simon cut across the social conventions. I take a long time to get to know people. Most young people won't sit down and talk for hours. Simon, though, found it easy to chat. He didn't strike me as a particularly shy person.

He seemed at ease at our house. Perhaps he found it easier to be bold and outgoing outside the home because he had several brothers and sisters.

I was very shocked and upset when Simon died. My strongest memory is hearing him clonk-clonk up the stairs in those big boots of his.
Mary Porter

I really miss Simon's unconventional ways and unique personality.

We had our differences. Throughout our midteens we saw eye to eye about very little. Simon had great difficulty coping with my values, which were so different from his. In our later teens, however, we developed more of a friendship.

Simon's death in many ways has brought me much closer to God. People have given reasons why Simon died. Some have said that he must have been walking out of God's will. Others have said, 'It's *our* fault. We never prayed enough.' But what God has shown me through all this is that he is sovereign. Nothing can happen unless he allows it.

Isn't it amazing when something so painful and tragic happens, God brings something so beautiful, unique and powerful? I'm still seeing and hearing of people whose lives have been changed as a direct result of Simon's death. Many people have been challenged to 'get up and go', to go for God in a new and real way.

Who knows when your time's up? Sometimes we see things from such a small perspective. Yet God's bigger than that. He's sovereign.

Daniel Reynolds, Simon's brother

In January 1994 I visited a church at Somerset West where Kobus Swart was speaking. I was really touched by the tears that he and Hazel and the others in the congregation shed even though Simon's funeral had been conducted three weeks previously.

Kobus said Simon had gone to a better place—heaven. To some extent, I envy him and wish I'd been ready to join Simon in our eternal home.

Africa has a great need for pioneers and bridgebuilders in a continent that has been divided for so many centuries. The violence and hardship that the people of Africa experience was certainly seen and ministered to by Simon. I commend his bridgebuilding work into townships.

I looked at the poem *Risk* that Simon adapted. Somehow Simon has been a seed that has died but will produce fruit. Later, on a visit to Bath, I went to buy a pair of shoes and ended up with some that looked more like boots in comparison with what I would normally buy. Someone remarked after Simon's memorial service that the boots at the front needed to be filled.

I want to be among those who say, 'I'm ready. I want to take up the challenge and the courage that Simon has demonstrated.' He was ready for the eternal glory which is given to all those who serve the Lord Jesus whole-heartedly.

Just before he died, Simon was considering working in Pietermaritzburg. I intend to go in his place. His death will inspire many people to work in these difficult and dangerous areas. Simon was a good flute player and I want to play the recorder. Simon was a Pied Piper. He led many with his joyous lifestyle.

I appreciate the sacrifice of the Reynolds family. Thanks to them for giving up their son for Africa. My hope is that many will follow Simon's example in bringing unity to Africa. May many people fill those boots and continue to walk the roads and townships with the good news.

Martin Schroeder, youth pastor,
Pietermaritzburg, South Africa

Simon, my son,
So young, so tall, so strong,
So full of hope, so unique,
So you.
Simon, part of my heart has been torn away.
Yet in that place of pain is also joy,
For I know that you stand with your eternal King,
Laughing and enjoying everything you believe in.

Simon, I remember your birth, your childhood,
Your youth and the beginning of manhood.
With laughter and tears, I remember those years.
These memories such sweet pearls to me now.

Simon, my heart is full of pride,
As I remember your life,
Especially as you set out to the land of your heart,
Bringing a message of hope and light,
Determined to show God's way is right.
Simon, you made a great preacher,
And, from what we hear, a pretty good bouncer!

Simon, my gentle giant,
So determined to be honest,
Determined not to follow the crowd.
You learnt what it meant
To follow Christ with no cop-out clause.

Simon, you made the world laugh.
And at times sometimes you drove them crazy!
Simon, always with a quest for truth,
You had plenty of difficult questions
And times when you doubted everything.

But when you found your truth,
You stood firm.

Simon, often my heart cries out for you,
Life, so fresh, just gone from us.
Sometimes the grief is overwhelming.
Yet in the darkness I find God's hand sustaining,
Bringing peace, comfort and such healing.

Simon, I'm so glad and proud
That you were my son.
Simon, I just wasn't prepared for this.
I never imagined this would ever be.
It's so hard to comprehend that you've gone.
But I stand and I'm not afraid,
Though sometimes I'm weak
And sometimes I tremble.
But I'm so glad that together
We share the glorious promise
That death cannot separate us from him.

Simon, one day a child, suddenly a man.
Simon, my first-born son.
Simon, not afraid to die.
Simon, I honour, I salute you.

Simon, with you gone
Part of my heart has flown away.
But this I know,
With joy and praise,
That one day
I will be as you are,
Praising our King
And rejoicing in his eternal presence
And care.

Sarah Manoehoetoe, written for Peter and Barbie Reynolds

To me, Simon draws a picture of a young man who was physically and spiritually 'head and shoulders above his fellows'. What he has accomplished in his short time here has been more than many twice his age.

John

One time we took the children from the church for a short holiday in the Mendip Hills. We planned to go on a night hike and sent the girls out to defend the bridge. Five minutes later the boys came out and the adults switched off the hut lights. It was a pitch black night. It was difficult even to see our hands in front of our faces.

The boys, including Simon, who was normally quite boisterous, became frightened and wouldn't budge. Eventually, after much persuasion they left the hut and made their way to the bridge. After about 45 minutes their eyes became accustomed to the dark and the boys' bravery returned.

Although Simon was one of the most frightened that evening, he certainly became a very brave man—a true explorer.

We were always impressed by the unconventional way Simon approached things and by his lack of fear in seemingly fearful situations, ultimately going into the townships to share the love of God. He was a man with a very big heart full of compassion and we will miss sharing in the excitement and courage with which he lived his life.

At the same time as his courage, he also had a wonderful gentleness which Diane experienced while he was assisting at Moorlands Infant School, Bath, as a 17-year-old. She loved watching him with the small children. He was so gentle and full of fun.

Nick and Di Stubbs, children's team leaders

I only met Simon once when he was kind enough to come and visit my eldest daughter, Rachel, when she was in hospital with measles. I was very grateful to him for his kindness.

Mavis Edmondson

Since Simon and our baby Timothy died, Dave and I have proved that God's grace is sufficient for whatever happens. But that doesn't mean we go around being afraid of what *might* happen.

There's much we don't understand. We've had to learn to trust God in a new way and know that he's in control, even when everything seems so out of control.

Simon was an ordinary person who decided to follow Jesus with everything in him. He set a good example of how to challenge what is unreal in our lives. Now I want to make the most of every minute I have on this earth.

I hope that in years to come it will be said of Simon, as was said of Abel: 'By faith he still speaks.'
Sarah Entwistle, Simon's sister

IGentle giant whose spirit was pure. Man who always left others room to make their own decisions. Man of peace, joy and a smiling face.
Trev Dunlop

He was the big brother I never had and, for a few years, my only true friend.
Julien Haycock

When I think of him I remember his lovely grin, curls and open, honest face. Every so often I'd bump into him at Beechen Cliff in Bath. He'd be praying as he looked across the city.
Mary Bunton

Simon was an excellent friend to have. He was just such a dude. His love of God and the way he lived his life was and is of great encouragement and inspiration to me.
Sheena Newland

What a challenge Simon's life has been and will continue to be! Pete particularly enjoyed his friendship and admired his outspokenness for the Lord. As with so many of the young people, his life and now his going to be with Jesus whom he loved so much has been a great challenge and example.
Chris and Pat Rogers

We always thought there was something big about him apart from his size. The poem you sent us only shows that he was a young spiritual giant. We'd already shed quite a few tears but this poem has deeply affected us all, especially our own fast-growing boys.
Wesley and Carol Richards

Simon was a great friend to me. He always lifted me up when I was down.
Alan Tancock

I picture him with that semi-shy, lopsided grin. I'm sure it has been a special time for you to be together in South Africa and to hear about his activities, exploits and mischief making from his friends.
Myra Keall

I remember his smile, his overflowing life and warmth and genuineness—and the crick in my neck! He was and is a very special person.
Alyssa Miller

I was so moved by Simon's poem *Risk* that I wanted to write it out. I hope you don't mind. My night school were all very moved by it when I used it as an example and I was able to share with them about your son. Another of my nonChristian friends read it and said, 'So that's what's wrong with my life?' I just wanted you to know how in some small way Simon is very obviously touching other people's lives.
Fiona Beavan

Joie de vivre, lust for life, happiness. Always up for a party. That's Simon in a nutshell. He was always happy to see everyone. Brilliant guy.
Beto Lopes, a barman at the hotel bar where Simon worked

I got to know him as a soft-hearted person who strove for peace. I'm the opposite in character in that I tend to react very quickly and make scenes of trivial things. He helped me in this. He was always saying, 'Eddy, don't let people disturb you. Don't let them take away your peace.'

He visited me regularly because we had a growing relationship. His love life is a secret, but what stands out was his honesty and moral values in his relationships with girls. There was a time I thought he would become my brother-in-law, but, oh, well . . .
Eddy Beukes, a gardener at Bizweni

I grew to love Simon deeply. I could start a conversation and he could finish it—without missing a beat!
Deon Briedenhann

Simon really crept into my heart and it was difficult to stay upset with him for any length of time. Like any young guy, he was insensitive and thoughtless at times— tracking mud all over my newly cleaned house or crashing noisily into the house at two in the morning after working at the bar. But he'd just look at me with this sheepish grin and all would be forgiven very quickly.

Unlike with other young guys, I could open my heart to Simon and share my problems with him. He'd always listen very carefully and would often say something that showed a wisdom far beyond his years. His insight was thoroughly unconventional. Deon and I would discuss together how we felt he had a great destiny ahead of him.

I believe Simon had an insight into God's sense of humour. He saw the funny side of most situations.

The other night I dreamed about an incident that happened while Simon was working for Deon. He was on a trip and was due back at about 12.30 that night. Deon and I were both lying in bed waiting for him to come in. I was relieved to hear the *bakkie* arrive and Simon's boots on the tiled floor. Then we heard a few other noises and scufflings and realised there must be someone else with him.

Then Simon called out, 'Hello. I've brought a friend to sleep the night.' We were quite puzzled, and were tickled the next morning to see Simon sleeping on the floor (as usual) and a little Coloured boy sleeping in his bed. We discovered that Simon had come across him pushing his bike along in the pitch black of night and had stopped to find out what was going on. (Typical of Simon. Most South Africans would just have driven past, thinking it was none of their business.)

The little boy, who lived with his grandparents, was on his way to his mother's on the west coast—about 250 km away. Fortunately, Deon was going down the west coast the next day and dropped the little guy off at his mother's. This is just one incident among many that I remember as it really touched me.

Another incident two weeks before he died touched and confronted us. Simon was chatting to a lady we know. She is trying to bring up three children on her own as her husband has left her. He managed to find out she had no money for food or even for toilet paper and shampoo. We'd been walking past her for days saying, 'How are you?' and her saying, 'Fine,' and we hadn't taken the time to find out how she really was.

Simon was down to his last few rand at the time, but he went to buy her toilet paper and other things she needed. This confronted other people who hadn't been aware of the situation. We managed to take up quite a sizeable collection to tide her through. One thing about Simon is that he always had time to talk to people and he never just looked at their outward appearance.

Erica Briedenhann

I found in Simon a happy person who was able to get involved with people, whether in the club where he worked, in the church or in the community.

Our friendship grew daily and I started missing him more the longer he stayed away. I felt that we as friends should spend more time together, but whenever I saw him with other people I realised he was the type of person who shared his friendship with everybody.

He showed me how to live and to love life: by giving to people today to receive from God tomorrow. In his death I received more life. I now live out what he lived for.

The *Risk* poem he wrote stays with me daily. I stuck it on the door of my wardrobe and whenever I open the door it's there to be read. I find the answer to my being in that poem. 'One of the greatest dangers in life is to risk nothing.'

Eugene Sitzer

What stood out about Simon to me was his strong personality. Yet he never intimidated people. He always had a word of encouragement.

Even though Simon was a big, tall guy, he had a soft heart. He'd always try to help where he could. He never felt out of place, no matter where he was or with whom.

Simon was one of the very few white people I knew who was able to look beyond colour and race. To him we were all equal.

173

Simon was a living example of a Christian. His death was for me the ultimate eye opener. I realised I couldn't just go on living for myself.

Anybody can ask me now: 'Do you love God? Do you have him in your life?' And my answer would be a definite, 'Yes!'

Beulah Januarie

Simon was a good and loyal friend who I was just getting to know.

He once said that the greatest negative in life is death. As Christians we had enough faith to believe that Jesus saved us from eternal death, so why should we be worried about it? Our problems, whatever they might be, are nothing compared to death.

During our visits to the black townships he won people's hearts, something few white men could accomplish.

Eben Louw

He related to me as his mother or grandmother. When he saw me walking, he always gave me a lift in the *bakkie,* even if it was close to my destination. He was always helpful and happy.

How did his death touch me? It was something very deep, because I'd become so used to him. He was like my child. It was something that hurt very much.

How will I manage without him? He treated me like a mother. When it rained, he mended my roof. He always visited me.

Auntie Louisa, Waterkloof squatter camp

He was a hell of a nice guy—more of a peacemaker than a bouncer.

Jean Joubert, fellow bouncer

I don't know if he really enjoyed working as a bouncer. He was a bit of a gentle giant. But with his height and his enormous boots, 99 times out of 100 there was no trouble.

People enjoyed his company. The business really picked up when he was around. That meant I didn't have a lot of time to socialise with him.

174

I think he knew where he was going. It was because of his way of life that he was so mature for his age.

John, owner of the hotel bar where Simon worked

Simon was a friend first and foremost. If there was something missing in my life he'd tell me. He was an easy person to talk with. It was only natural for him to accept people because he didn't have any preconceived ideas about them. He never spoke negatively about others and was uneasy in the company of people who did.

It was remarkable the way he used his relating to people, his love of music and his poetry, combined with his unique personality, to tell friends about God in his unorthodox way.

There was a rich wisdom that emanated from him, a wisdom far above that normal for a 21-year-old. It was great just to listen to him. I have to add that he also could talk a lot of rubbish. He'd come up with, 'Have you ever thought that maybe we're not really existing? Maybe we're just an idea in God's mind.'

For a long time we'd been praying for something to happen in the area of relating between the young people at Bizweni. Now I realise Simon was that gift from God, that answer to prayer, that thing that made the way for us to break down walls, to relate with one another in more freedom and love. He prepared the path in our social circle for the move of God that's happening now.

Kobus Swart, church leader in South Africa

I was really privileged to know him, even for such a short while. His life spoke loads, but I think his leaving has really awakened me to let my life mean something. I'm so excited!

I came across a card in a shop that I'd have loved to give to Simon. It read: 'If life was a jukebox, you'd be a gold record.'

Sandy Lopes

I was drawn to Simon by his sense of humour and light-heartedness. He was tall enough to make a cheeky remark to our boss and get away with it. He endeared us all by his cocktail of diligent work when required and his sense of fun. This relieved our frustrations and anxieties when needed.

Although I wasn't involved with his church activities, I spent time outside of work with Simon and some of his friends. Simon was always organising something out of the ordinary. One minute we might be having a drink together in the pub, the next minute a group of us would be larking about on the top of Solsbury Hill.

Simon must have headed the *Wayne's World* fan club. He could quote most of the classic lines which, to me, became his trademark. Blending his sense of humour and slight American accent, you were almost in the film.

Simon left work after a long campaign to raise funds for a ticket to South Africa. All at the company were sad to see him go, but happy that he was doing something he'd talked about doing for a long time.

Now we miss him more than ever.

Steve Nash, Acer Engineering

Simon made himself comfortable very quickly and he had the kids doing things for him in no time. It wasn't long after that when he had Avril doing things for him, too. I tried to make him as uncomfortable as possible to try to maintain a balance and keep him in reality. I was always outnumbered because, as he once said to me, 'Be nice, Mark. Everyone else likes me.'

I was amazed at how at home Simon was with God. He wasn't put off by difficult questions by my cousin John Mark, who was the same age as Simon. He had a way of making the questioner question his questions.

Simon always laughed easily at things, others, circumstances and himself. He opened my eyes to many things regarding the young black men working on the farm. He had none of the prejudice I was brought up with and was free to discuss anything with any one of them. He told me of their personal hopes, dreams, perceptions of the boss and white people. Simon showed me how to take a person as an individual and not indulge in sweeping generalisations, particularly with regard to race and colour.

He would assist in the harvesting, turned a wonderful salmon pink in the December sun. He resorted to copious applications of sunscreen, which served to capture the dust and turned him into a gingerbread man.

It was also found necessary for him to have a very large red handkerchief around his neck. After a few days Simon was at one with his handkerchief.

I found Simon refreshing, challenging and frustrating, especially if I came off second best in our continuous repartee. I also came to love him a great deal, as did Avril my wife, Douglas, Ruth, Joanna and Stephen. We were looking forward to his visiting us again this January and somehow feel robbed and a deep sense of loss.

He was an accomplished correspondent, things like, 'Today I'm ill, probably 'cos of your letter, so I've taken the day off,' and, 'Say hi to John Mark. Tell him I pray for him, too. Tell him to stop trying to run away from God. Only a mindless weasel would do that, 'cos God's a faster runner.'

Mark Bird

When he first came to us, we arranged to meet Simon at church one Sunday and bring him up to the farm to visit and help. The first thing that went through my mind was, 'How am I going to feed him? He's even taller than Mark!' It really shouldn't have been a concern. He ate everything at any time, in any quantity.

The one thing Simon didn't like was good old South African rusks, which in our home is like a staple diet. If anyone is hungry it's a rusk dunked in tea. In a letter from Simon in England this is what he thought of rusks, 'One thing I don't miss is rusks. How can you *eat* those things? Every house I stayed in Africa I was severely tormented by mothers who would tantalisingly try to persuade me to eat "just one". They taste like crusts of prehistoric bread.'

For his second visit Simon decided to bunk for a week. Instead of flying straight to Kobus, he flew to Durban to spend a week or so on the farm. He said he knew he was to stay in the Cape for about a year and really wanted to spend some time with us before settling in the Cape.

It was a typically hot, humid Natal day, with the temperature at about 30 degrees, when I fetched him from the airport. Simon must have had on all his winter clothes—coat, scarf, you name it, he had it on. 'How could I possibly have fitted all my tapes in if I hadn't worn all my clothes?' he asked.

He was a precious young man, a privilege to know, for parents with four young children a wonderful example. A mature young man who shared from his heart so openly.

Avril Bird

When I first met Simon he was different from the start, like no one I've met before. Soon after he arrived in South Africa he set off from my house walking to Woodcutters. No one does that here, let alone arrive with someone he met along the way. But that was the type of guy Simon was. It didn't matter to him that this guy was homeless and down on his back. In fact, Simon wouldn't even have seen those aspects of him.

Imagine the scene. In walks this talk 6'7" boy with his 'new' friend. This is how genuine Simon was. When I arrived in London he felt like a brother to me. He reprimanded me for not calling sooner and welcomed me to Bath with his characteristic enthusiasm. I could talk to him about anything and he took me everywhere.

Natasha van Niekerk

We knew Simon and, though our encounter was brief, we couldn't but be affected by his winning ways with children and his love for them. Roscoe was especially impressed by Simon and really enjoyed the time spent in his company.

Great rejoicing filled our hearts on the evening of 31 May when little Joel Simon joined the d'Souza family. We named him 'Joel', as that was the name given to Brenda by the Lord, and 'Simon', in honour of Simon Reynolds.

He was a brave and courageous young man whom we loved and admired, though from afar.

Zephry d'Souza, church leader in Jaipur, North India

Every so often on the horizon of the history of mankind there arises a person or a family who are the delightful moldbreakers of conformity. They are like a fresh breeze blowing through the cobwebs of tradition. They leave us gasping for breath as we excitedly encounter their lives.

Simon as a person was like that. His life can be likened to a mysterious song.

There was the 'laughing troubadour' tune that he played. I remember an encounter of his with an old lady of 80 years old. Simon had gone to pick her up to bring her to my home. But on the way back they got lost. This was the old lady's first encounter with Simon. I went and asked her what the experience was like. She looked at me as if casting her mind back and said, 'Both of us just laughed and laughed.' It was delightful, she said. That old lady was my mother. She had been touched by the tune of the laughing troubadour.

If he did those type of things on earth, what in heaven will he be doing now? Hiding the angels' incense bowls? Swapping Moses' halo for Israel's? Adjusting the angelic choir notes? I can hardly wait to hear of his escapades across the river of visibility!

Then there was his ability to give new meaning to old things. Pictured vividly in front of me are Simon's boots. If any shoes could talk, would they tell us of the time when both of us prayed for you all as a family? When he gave new meaning to thankfulness, telling me of his appreciation of his mum and dad through all the difficulties of growing up and trying to find his own notes, in a Christianity that had grown a long white beard of conformity and religiosity?

Would those boots tell of his visits to the black townships, and the times when he reached out to the hidden Christ in the visible poor? Would they tell us of the police wanting to pick up this tall, strange white man in an area regarded as highly dangerous?

And what of the money he gave to the needy which gained its value even the more as it was freely given away? Would those boots tell of visiting old people, of visiting pubs and giving new meaning to witnessing? How beautiful are the boots of Simon, on the hills of Richmond and Durban and on the plains of the Cape.

Jim Eliot once said: 'He is no fool who gives what he cannot keep to gain what he cannot lose.' This is an unusual tune today. In a day when he could have chosen the luxury of staying at home and being reliant on the dole, Simon chose the tune of coming to work in a country being raped with the violence of racism and tribalism.

In a day when the youth are thinking only of themselves, he thought of us in Africa.

Peter van Niekerk, church leader in South Africa

Simon loved life and was deeply sensitive. He loved the unlovely, identifying with the homeless and the outcasts of society. He liberated people to accept their own humanity.

I enjoyed his ordinariness and his respect for people, no matter who they were. If he was talking to a little child he would give that child the same attention he would give to an adult.

I never felt threatened by his size. He never dominated the room, even though he was so tall. He wasn't quick to give up his convictions until God spoke to him about them.

When I get to heaven I'm going to give him a kick up the butt and say, 'How did you get here before me?'

Shoba Holly

We are grateful for the individual and personal friendship we enjoy with each of our children.

We miss Simon deeply. We miss the long conversations with him. We miss his wonderful smile and being able to hug his 6'7" frame. But we will see him again. Our greatest joy is that he is with Jesus, the one he loved the most.

Psalm 127:3-4 declares: 'Children [are] . . . like arrows in the hand of a warrior.' It has been a privilege to have been Simon's parents. We are encouraged at the potential in each of our childeren to make an impact for God—to be his instrument to love and serve others. Our prayer is that the emerging generation will, like arrows, go far beyond our own.

'To live is Christ and to die is gain' (Philippians 1:21).

Peter & Barbie Reynolds, Simon's parents

Working at the bar

Alastair worked as a bouncer with Simon at the hotel bar. In his colourful language he described what it was like working with him:

When he started there he quizzed me about what the job was like. 'We're not going to act like thugs, are we?' he asked, concerned.

'No,' I assured him.

He and I used to laugh at other blokes who acted like Rambo when they walked in.

Simon was a very brave guy. Like in anything, if you've never been in that situation before, it takes a lot of guts.

The first night at 1.30 am I said, 'Nothing's gonna happen tonight.' Just as I said it, four or five big guys started beating the shit out of each other. Simon was right there. It went on for a while until we dragged the whole lot outside and there was a bit of a fight. It turned out they were off-duty policemen!

Sometimes Simon would ask a guy to leave and get the response: 'I'll go when my beer's finished.'

Simon would down his beer for him, then say, 'Your beer's finished. Now out!'

I wasn't there when he hurt his hand the first time. The people going there were low-life shit. Some real mean people, and this one guy attacked Simon. He was drunk and pushed Simon away. When he came for him again, Simon hit him, hurting his own hand.

I was at the bar next door. When I got there Simon was standing, holding him. Because of the way the Hole is situated we had to drag them out a block away. And a mob always followed the guy. This guy went for me, and even though Simon's hand was broken he slapped him away.

After working for the weekend, Simon and Alastair would sometimes go out together on Sunday night, visiting a nightclub or a friend's house.

When I was moving to the apartment, he was the only person who helped me move. I wouldn't have been able to do it without him.

Thinking back, I'd describe Simon as genuine and decent.

Once a guy put his face close to Simon's and said, 'I'm going to f . . . you up.'

Simon was his usual self, starting to put the guy down, but not in a horrible way.

The guy would say, 'I'm going to bust your teeth in for you.'

Simon would say, 'And the nose? What are you going to do about the nose? I hear it's really painful.'

Another time when Simon was on duty alone, all hell broke lose. This guy didn't want to take his hat off when Simon asked him. He got all his friends together and Simon was standing alone with 10 guys in front of him. He always had this habit of eating biltong (beef sticks) and would put them in his jeans back pocket.

Well, when he saw these 10 guys in front of him he put the beef stick he was chewing into his back pocket. The guy thought he was pulling a revolver out and ran away.

Later Simon became friends with the guy and said to him, 'Do you realise I scared you off with a beef stick?'

If a girl in tight pants walked by I'd be eyeing her and I'd tell Simon, but he wasn't interested. The only offers he'd get were from the disgusting things that crawled out of the bar. He never had a romantic thing with the girls there. He wasn't disgusting like I was.

A few of the girls who worked there liked him and when I told him he'd say: 'What?' and just shrug it off. I think it was because he'd quite often save them from guys who'd come on to them or were pushy with them. And then they'd think, 'Oh, Simon. My hero!'

Kirsten, Alastair's girlfriend, said about Simon, 'I think the girls liked him because he was decent. I mean, Simon was the kind of guy who'd make a good husband. I couldn't see anyone wanting to hurt Simon. He was so honest. He was always friendly and would go out of his way to help you.'

Alastair saw yet another side to Simon off duty:

Simon enjoyed a good joke. I remember one night this woman came up to me and said, 'I believe you're a great dancer.' I told her I didn't know how to dance but she persisted. I looked across at Simon, who was pissing himself with laughter.

Apparently this woman had come up to him and asked him to dance. Simon said he didn't know how to dance but that guy over there (me) was a great dancer and had even won prizes for his dancing. But if she came and asked me to dance, I'd say I didn't know how to dance. 'Don't believe him,' Simon had told her.

When he started permanent work at the bar he told me he'd go through all this shit every night and then afterwards he'd be chased by dogs and be scared, having to run all the way home!

I remember one time when he had the painting job there were a few cuts on his hand. The thinners got into the cuts and he put mercuro-chrome on them. This made them look something awful. Simon came up behind this guy sitting at the bar who was causing shit and put his hand on his shoulder.

This guy saw Simon's hand looking like something that was hanging on a meat hook, he looked up into Simon's chest and then looked up again into Simon's face towering over him. The guy didn't give him any more problems!

Me and Simon were actually damn good friends. After Simon died I said to this friend I work with: 'I'm really pissed off because you go to funerals and everyone says, "He was such a nice guy." Meantime they're such assholes. But in Simon's case it was so true.'

Did Simon ever talk to me about God? Not a lot. He didn't need to. Simon showed us how to live—and I just wanted to be like him.

Postscript

To laugh is to risk looking a fool.
To weep is to risk appearing sentimental.
To reach out for another is to risk involvement.

To show feelings is to risk revealing your true self.
To place your ideas and dreams before a crowd is to
*   risk their loss.*

To love is to risk rejection.
To live is to risk dying.
To hope is to risk despair.
To try is to risk failure.

But risks must be taken,
Because one of the greatest dangers in life is to risk
*   nothing.*
Those who risk nothing do nothing, achieve nothing
*   and become nothing.*
They may avoid suffering and sorrow,
But they cannot learn, feel, change, grow, love or even
*   live.*
Chained by their uncertainties, they are slaves.
They have forfeited their freedom.
Only a person who risks all that he cannot keep,
To gain what he can never lose,
Is truly free.

It was almost five months after Simon's death. Two former enemies, F W de Klerk and Nelson Mandela, stood side by side. Mandela's black arm was raised in salute as he welcomed the new presidential post. Holding his hand up for the world to see was the former white president of South Africa, smiling and welcoming a new day for South Africa. That day, 10 May 1994, was a momentous occasion. It would have thrilled Simon.

Nelson Mandela's rise to become president was an achievement that amazed critics and supporters alike. Within months, African people in Bloemfontein were dancing and chanting on the deposed statue of Dr Hendrick Verwoerd, the architect of apartheid.

It was 16 December 1994, the first anniversary of Simon's death. The Day of the Vow—which stood for all that was evil about apartheid—was mourned by a handful of diehard Afrikaners at the Voortrekker Monument, Pretoria. The 1000 attenders were not converts to the African National Congress. They sang the old Afikaner anthem *Die Stem* rather than the new national anthem *Nkosi Sikelele Afrika*. But the old right-wing rhetoric was gone and there was instead a spirit of reconciliation in the air.

One Afrikaner woman sang the hymns while carrying a black child in her arms. Observers commented that it was in the same vein as the first commemoration of Blood River in 1864, which was attended by a delegation of Zulu warriors.

Meanwhile, in South Africa at large, the Day of the Vow had been changed by Nelson Mandela to the Day of Reconciliation, marking the date in 1990 when F W de Klerk announced the lifting of apartheid. An amnesty on weapons of destruction was declared and thousands of guns used in the armed struggle were being willingly handed in by people of all races as a clear demonstration of peaceful co-existence.

Second Vice-President F W de Klerk, leader of the National Party and South Africa's former president, commented: 'Afikaners need not despair. The future lies in joint citizenship and peaceful coexistence. We believe our values will not only survive, but will continue to play a benevolent role in the new rainbow nation.'

Among other traditional South African public holidays now abolished include Republic Day on 31 May, which celebrated South Africa's decision in 1961 to quit the Commonwealth. South Africa at last was changing.

As the sun comes up in the skies of war
And the moon fades out of sight,
The rains in Africa fall no more,
But the sun still burns too bright.
The children are dying of starvation.
Listen to their cries.
Hear the plea of a starving nation
As another baby dies.

As they all unite to form a New Age
They usher in the Beast.
But one thing they don't understand
Is you can't kill for peace!
In China they're killing for moral belief.
In Africa they starve.
Ethiopia's showered with famine relief,
But the population's halved.

Hopelessness dwells in a young girl's eyes
As she plays in the gutter alone.
Her future is built on corruption and lies
As she searches for hope and a home.
The fear of death in a young man's mind
Is one he will conceal,
But to kill for a peace that he won't find
Is a nightmare all too real.

Where is the answer to this dying place?
Who can show us the way?
One Man came with abundance of grace
And he's still in the business today.
His answer is not in what he can gain,
But rather in what he can give.
This Man once died, but rose again,
In order that we can live.

Simon Nathan Reynolds 1972-93

Siomon would have rejoiced to see the new South Africa continue to emerge from the ashes of apartheid and repression. Not only would he have seen a partial fulfilment of his life's mission against injustice, but he would have joined South Africans of all races celebrating in the streets the new South Africa.

'Who will fill these boots?'

Profits from the sale of this book will go to the Simon Reynolds Youth Fund to support youth work in South Africa. Additional donations to the fund can be sent to:

Simon Reynolds Youth Fund
1a Forum Buildings
Bath
Avon BA1 1UG
UK